The Soul: Understanding Our Real Identity

The Key to Spiritual Awakening

Stephen Knapp

Dedicated to all seekers of deep spiritual truth.

Writing this book was such a kick for me because it brought me back to the early days when I first started studying this spiritual information, and to the books which first began to open my eyes. I would be upstairs in my room, reading and pondering away, going through so many internal changes and realizations. I felt like after all the previous religious studying I had done in Church and in the philosophies from around the world, I was now finally getting somewhere significant. I felt like I was finally being privileged to the secret knowledge that would open my eyes to reality, a level of perception that I had not found before. There is no doubt that it changed my life forever. And that is what I am hoping this book can provide for you.

Copyright © 2010, by Stephen Knapp

All rights reserved. No part of this book may be reproduced without written permission from the copyright owner and publisher, except for brief quotations for review or educational purposes.

ISBN: 1453733833

EAN: 9781453733837

Cover graphic: Aquarian Awakening, the Perfection © by Jack Hass, from www.celestial-art.net.
Visionary digital art intended to help transform us inwardly into the cosmic, unbound and divine beings we truly are. To me, this represents the multiple potencies of the living being, or the soul.

Other books by the author:
1. The Secret Teachings of the Vedas: The Eastern Answers to the Mysteries of Life
2. The Universal Path to Enlightenment
3. The Vedic Prophecies: A New Look into the Future
4. How the Universe was Created and Our Purpose In It
5. Toward World Peace: Seeing the Unity Between Us All
6. Facing Death: Welcoming the Afterlife
7. The Key to Real Happiness
8. Proof of Vedic Culture's Global Existence
9. The Heart of Hinduism: The Eastern Path to Freedom, Enlightenment and Illumination
10. The Power of the Dharma: An Introduction to Hinduism and Vedic Culture
11. Vedic Culture: The Difference it can Make in Your Life
12. Reincarnation & Karma: How They Really Affect Us
13. The Eleventh Commandment: The Next Step for Social Spiritual Development
14. Seeing Spiritual India: A Guide to Temples, Holy Sites, Festivals and Traditions
15. Crimes Against India: And the Need to Protect its Ancient Vedic Tradition
16. Destined for Infinity, a spiritual adventure in the Himalayas
17. Yoga and Meditation: Their Real Purpose and How to Get Started
18. Avatars, Gods and Goddesses of Vedic Culture: Understanding the Characteristics, Powers and Positions of the Hindu Divinities

You can find out more about
Stephen Knapp
and his books, free ebooks, research,
and numerous articles and photos,
along with many other spiritual resources at:
http://www.Stephen-Knapp.com

CONTENTS

INTRODUCTION   1

CHAPTER ONE   2
YOU ARE MORE THAN YOUR BODY

CHAPTER TWO   8
IGNORANCE OF THE SOUL, THE BASIS OF ILLUSION
    The Prime Reason for Suffering * Wrong Attachments * The Misguided Aim of Life * All Suffering Exists Only Within the Illusion

CHAPTER THREE   29
THE PURPOSE OF LIFE

CHAPTER FOUR   37
THE PATH OF REALIZATION
    The Supreme Occupation and Highest Bliss

CHAPTER FIVE   52
HOW THE SOUL IS ETERNAL
    Seeing the Big Picture

CHAPTER SIX   61
THE SIZE AND NATURE OF THE SOUL

CHAPTER SEVEN   67
THE SUPERSOUL

CHAPTER EIGHT   75
SPIRITUAL PERCEPTION

CHAPTER NINE LIFE AFTER DEATH	83
CONCLUSION	89
GLOSSARY	90
REFERENCES	98
INDEX	102
ABOUT THE AUTHOR	105

INTRODUCTION

The idea that we are more than merely these material bodies is pervasive. It is found in every religion and spiritual path in this world. However, many religions only hint at the details of this knowledge, but if we look around we will find that practically the deepest and clearest descriptions of the soul and its characteristics are found in the Vedic texts of India. There is a vast amount of such information that they offer from many different angles of understanding.

In this book, however, I am providing the much needed information but without going into all the details that have been described or outlined in the Vedic texts. If I were to provide every verse or description that is given in the Vedic literature on this topic, you would likely become overwhelmed with all the information, and this would be a much larger volume. So, I am writing an introductory book, a summarization of the most essential spiritual knowledge that will give you the seeds to spiritual enlightenment, a new and deeper look at who you really are as a spiritual being. This will give you the basics from which you can continue to research and find more details that can help clarify your understanding of this topic.

If you like this book, then you may also want to read my book *The Secret Teachings of the Vedas*, which I wrote as a further step and in-depth guide to understanding this knowledge on a much deeper and more comprehensive level. Other books of your choice that will help in this matter are also listed in the back of this book.

CHAPTER ONE

You Are More than Your Body

The first thing in understanding your spiritual identity is to perceive that you are more than just your physical body. You are the spiritual essence within the body. You are the spark of consciousness which keeps the body alive and working. You are merely wearing your body like an outfit, a spacesuit that is suitable for living on this particular planet.

It is like a driver in a car. You drive the car wherever you want to go with it, but you are not the car, only the driver within. You decide and direct what is to be done with it. But often when there is an auto accident, when one car hits another, the driver of the struck car gets out and says "You hit me" to the other driver. Yet, actually it was the car that was struck, not necessarily the driver. Of course, if it was a bad accident, the drivers may also be affected and injured, but the primary damage is usually to the car. Similarly, our body is the primary vehicle in which we are temporarily existing, and through which we are experiencing this life.

This does not mean that the body and our present life are not important. They are both extremely important, because where we go from this lifetime depends on how we live this life, and how we use this body. It depends on how we develop ourselves. This body is important because it is the vehicle by which we learn about this realm of existence, and through which we cultivate what kind of consciousness we have:

material or spiritual, or some of both. And that is what will steer us in the direction we take after we leave this body. This is what we must learn in this life.

Every religion and every culture has some information about our spiritual identity. They all teach you to pay attention to the spiritual identity within you, and they provide some instructions on how to do that and the reasons for doing so. This is primarily based on the fact that this life is impermanent, your body is temporary, but your spiritual identity, the soul, is permanent. It is the constant factor in all that happens to you, whether good or bad. It is the real you, and the sooner we can realize and perceive that, the sooner we can understand our true potential of who and what we really are, and what we can accomplish in this life. This is the essence of what we find in many religions.

For example, as the Bible explains: "The sensual man perceiveth not the things that are of the Spirit of God, for it is foolishness to him, and he cannot understand it. A man who is unspiritual refuses what belongs to the Spirit of God; it is folly to him; he cannot grasp it, because it needs to be judged in the light of the Spirit." (*I Corinthians*.2.14)

This means that when the level of intelligence is small, or the ability in humanity to perceive the spiritual is not very deep, then how can they understand or comprehend such knowledge? As in the case of Jesus, he was not able to teach all he had to offer because of the crudeness of the people of that time and area. At one point he said: "I have yet many things to say unto you, but you cannot bear them now." (*John* 16.12) Even what he did say caused such a reaction that it was eventually arranged that he be killed. So, it is obvious that only so much knowledge can be given to certain people at certain times, according to their ability to understand.

As Jesus further stated: "If you do not believe when I tell you of material things, how will you believe when I tell you of spiritual things?" (*John* 3.12) This is actually what Jesus and all teachers of the law of God have to deal with: a lack of faith and understanding amongst the people in general. Therefore, Jesus often spoke in parables whereby those who were ignorant of the law would hear only a simple, moralistic story, while the advanced initiates would understand the deeper meaning within. But Jesus also said: "These things have I spoken to you in proverbs; but the time cometh when I shall show you of the Father." (*John* 16.25) This meant that there was more knowledge to come and such knowledge would clearly describe the deeper aspects of the Absolute Truth.

As anyone can see by reading the Bible, very little information is offered that directly describes God or the soul, or even the relationship between them. Christians do not have a clear concept of who and what is God. At best, God is described as almighty, great, angry, greatly to be feared, the ever-lasting Father, the alpha and omega, etc. In the Old Testament, God is described as appearing as a dove, a pillar of fire by night, a cloud by day, a burning bush, and so on. But this says nothing of His bodily features, His opulences, His abode, His activities, or exactly how He creates and manifests the material and spiritual worlds. Therefore, Jesus said there would be more knowledge to receive. But are Christians really ready to receive it? Most of them feel they have all they need, thus, disregarding the very instructions of Jesus.

In fact, the Bible agrees with the idea of researching other scripture for answers, because in *II Timothy* (3.16-17) we find the following quote: "All scripture is given by inspiration of God, and is profitable for doctrine, for reproof, for correction, for instruction in righteousness, that the man of God may be perfect, thoroughly furnished in all good works." So, it is without a doubt that all scripture everywhere is meant to uplift our consciousness, and can be used by anyone.

Therefore, in most of the conventional and Western scriptures, we have little understanding of what is the soul and how to actually perceive it as our spiritual identity. But throughout the scriptures of the world we find hints as to what it is, and that it is eternal. And being eternal, if we follow virtue properly, we should regain our rightful place back in the service of God. For example, in the *Koran* (9.112) we find it said that those who turn to God in repentance and serve and praise Him, and engage in devotion to God, who bow down and pray, who do good and avoid evil, will rejoice. So proclaim these glad tidings to the believers. Then we also find it said (19.65) that everyone should worship the Lord of the heavens and the earth and be patient in constant worship. For who is worthy of the same name as God?

In Zoroastrianism it is believed that a person must live according to the religious tenets if one hopes to joyfully go before the Creator in the next world. The best of all practices is the worship of God, for all are servants of God. So, one must lead a righteous life since it is one's thoughts, words, and deeds that determine one's next life after death. Similarly, in Sikhism we find the precept that a true follower serves the Supreme Soul alone.

Therefore, as we can see from this little sampling, many such quotes can be found in various scriptures, including many from the Christian and Jewish traditions, that give credence to understanding our spiritual identity, and which mention the need for devotion to God as the means to realize our spiritual position.

Actually, we could go on quoting varieties of texts in this way to verify their views that we are all souls within this material body, though we may still not know quite what it is from these descriptions. However, aside from this, there is also the point that the soul is eternal, and, thus, subject to reincarnation, or developing oneself over the course of many lifetimes. For example, the Jewish book the *Zohar* mentions that for the living beings to return to the Absolute, they must develop all the perfections, which if not done in one life must be accomplished in a second, third, or however many lifetimes is necessary to attain reunion with God. The *Cabala* (or *Kabbala*), which is a very important book amongst Hebraic scholars, also has information about past and future lives.

The Buddhist and Taoist scriptures also contain much information about rebirth. In fact, all over the world you can find the idea of reincarnation mentioned in many ancient customs and texts. This was also found in the philosophy of the Gallic Druids, African Zulus, Eskimos of Greenland, North American Indians such as the Hopi, the Dayaks of Borneo, Karens of Burma, and even the natives of New Guinea. So, this is nothing new, but not every scripture provides this knowledge in much depth. Thus, some scriptures and cultures offer more complete spiritual knowledge than others.

One thing to understand is that each religion or spiritual path in this world is different in three ways, namely the time in history in which it appeared, the location where it developed, and the people who were taught. According to these three factors, different levels of knowledge were given. In other words, if the people of the time and location were not spiritually capable of understanding deep knowledge, not as much information would or could be given. What was provided would have to be given in a most simplified manner, such as in proverbs, parables, or something like that. However, where people were used to thinking in more complex manners, then deeper spiritual knowledge could be and was provided. This can be seen in the Eastern or Vedic culture of India, in which the spiritual knowledge that was available was much more specific, and more descriptive about our spiritual identity than other religions.

Therefore, if we really want to get to the heart of the matter, then we have to look for and use those spiritual texts which offer the clearest knowledge and deepest understanding that we can find. And throughout all of my research, I have found none that did this more effectively and gave the most illumination in this regard than the ancient Vedic texts of the region of India. So, let us have a look at how they can help us understand who and what we really are.

CHAPTER TWO

Ignorance of the Soul The Basis of Illusion

When you think you are this body, or that your body is your real identity, and you are absorbed in body consciousness, it can be the cause of much confusion and misdirected aims in life. This is the problem. It can also be the cause of many inappropriate feelings, like jealousy, lust, anger, hatred, and so on, which only come into being if one is convinced that they are the body and the happiness or pleasure of the body and senses is the main purpose in life.

The fact is that we are all born into ignorance. Thus, we come into this world not knowing who and what we really are, and we need to find out. However, as it is today, the whole process of education is to provide the knowledge we need to know so we can function in this world. We need to know how to spell, read, write, do arithmetic, and comprehend and work in this world, at least to provide ourselves with the means to survive the many challenges that will come our way in this life. Then we grow, learn a trade or something, contribute to society in some way, then produce children, stay for some time, and then dwindle and die. Then that is the end of it all. Or is it?

After all that, what have we really accomplished during that time? Have we only accepted ourselves as a material being, a product of this material world? Or is there something more? Is there something we are missing? That is the problem with modern education: it keeps you focused on the idea that you are merely the body, mind and senses, and gives you the means to maintain them and engage in material society, economics, career development, etc., only for maintaining the body and pursuing the happiness of the mind and senses. Therefore, are we only given enough information to think that we have the freedom of choice in what we do with ourselves, or do we merely function according to the dictates, the indoctrination of other authorities? What is the real purpose of this world anyway? Are we more than we appear to be? There seems to be little knowledge in the mainstream that allows us to seriously look at who we really are.

Does this world consist of only what we see, hear, touch, smell, and taste? Are we expected to accept that all that is real is only what we can see? Or are there multi dimensions that exist both within and around us that we should understand? Is this world only for allowing us to work in a system that keeps us bound to the so-called freedom of continuing to work hard for money? Is this really life, or is this slavery that has been devised by those in higher positions who contrive to receive the majority of benefits? Are the choices of lifestyle decreasing as the years go by? Or are we lead into a system of living like a heard of sheeple that are expected to work hard and remain docile under any circumstance? Are we indoctrinated in a way that makes us believe we have to accept whatever food, medicine, pharmaceuticals, or economic systems that are pushed on us, along with the dictates of big government whether we like it or not? Where is the means to live a life of peace and happiness the way we would like? Or are we expected to live without doing too much thinking about all of this? Are we expected to use our lives to merely work hard, pay taxes and be dull-headed beasts of burden that are relieved or distracted from our troubles through the preoccupation of television, food that is no longer nutritious, drugs that turn us into zombies, and the ever-present desires for sex that are perpetuated and even ignited by the media, advertisements that tell us what we should want, and the scenarios presented in the entertainment world? Is this all that this life and this increasingly polluted world supposed to be? Or is there more to it than that? Is there more information about it that is being kept from us?

Was there an ancient time when there was knowledge available that could tell us what is the real purpose of life and this world? And can we still find this knowledge today? And not merely information about it, but also the process that can open our eyes, open our consciousness to actually see the truth? See what is this world, and who and what we really are?

This is the information that is becoming more difficult to find, especially amongst all of our preoccupations to solve our material problems, or all the academics who give their intellectual and speculative views on the purpose of life, or all the religions that say they are the only way and all others are but paths to hell, even though most of them have such little knowledge to offer about God and the soul, but will be sure to tell you all the ways of the devil and how you are hell-bound without their help.

How is it, amongst all of this, are we really supposed to discern the truth and free ourselves to perceive the reality within ourselves, that which can withstand the tests of time and not be shaped according to the ever-changing attitudes and persuasions of the faulty views of men and their fickle dispositions? Where is the truth that can take us out of being slaves to this holographic world, where everything has a beginning, middle and end, but instead reach that realm which is steady, balanced and eternal? Are we only supposed to accept this world of temporary appearances? Or is there a way to understand how to get beyond this illusion? That is what is to be known, understood, realized, perceived, and experienced. And that is not impossible.

Ignorance of the Soul

The information that answers these questions and was given to humanity many years ago is still found in the ancient texts of the East, and from those sages who still practice and understand them. That is where you can find the truth of the purpose of life and the reality of your real identity. That is what can lead you to perceive what is real in this ever-changing world.

Some people, of course, are so attached to the illusion, to who and what they think their material identity is, that they will even fight to justify their continued participation in it. They will fight to protect it, as if in an army led by the orders of those who are in positions of power and authority who can easily manipulate those entrenched in the illusion and its false system of existence. Blind to anything else, such people remain confident that they will never be lead in the wrong direction by their governments, or religious, educational, or even business establishments. But if you can see beyond the veil of appearances, it is all but a means of control over the lower people by the higher oligarchy. This is because when such administrations have foundations based on materialism and the addiction of acquiring more converts and more power, they will never be able to bring in or raise you to higher levels of thought and consciousness. It is to their advantage to keep you in ignorance, offering you only the apparent freedom of thinking you have a choice in how your lives are directed, yet making sure that all such choices made are but dictated to you. And sometimes when you cannot correct the system, the best thing is to simply go around it, or rise above it, by a flood of spiritual knowledge throughout the masses. Thus, those who are open to it can begin to see the difference between truth and illusion. They can begin to awaken from a foggy consciousness, awaken from the dream. Spreading this spiritual knowledge is the duty of those who understand it, to provide freedom from the illusion.

The illusion, meaning the materialistic consciousness, is what keeps a person absorbed in a system that keeps the body, mind and senses preoccupied with a superficial existence. It keeps one from understanding spiritual reality, or, in many cases, from having the time or even being interested in it. Thus, attachment to this illusion makes one more easily manipulated by the false promise of sensual reward and mental pleasure if one stays entrenched in this system. It is like a vicious circle of continuing to work hard for the freedom of continuing to work hard for what is little reward, while giving most of the fruits of your labor, hopes and dreams to those who remain in control, or willing to exploit you to the maximum, though you are hardly aware of it. It is like a donkey, working so hard, decreasing its duration of life, giving all of his labor to his master, while being given only a few handfuls of grass for its reward. Now is that some kind of life worth living, a life to be proud of?

Naturally, work of some kind is always necessary. One must live by means of some occupation, but the ideal is to engage in simple living and high thinking. This means that we work to maintain ourselves in a simple way, but also to become free from the illusion through the cultivation of spiritual knowledge, and spend time in spiritual practices that open our consciousness to a higher perception of life. Then life has real meaning because it deals with reality, with what and who you really are as a spiritual being rather than merely as a material body. This is the purpose of human life. This is the difference between the life of a human and that of an ordinary beast of burden, or any other animal. But the question you must ask yourself is which one do you really want to be?

Freedom from the illusion also means to be free of all the usual limitations, difficulties and challenges that one normally faces in this material realm, or at least to see them from an alternative and uplifting point of view, and to be open to all the limitless potential and possibilities that become available when one realizes his or her true spiritual identity. Such freedom can only be attained when you raise your consciousness to see your real spiritual form, to realize your true self, and see who you are beyond the illusion. This is accomplished by cultivating deep spiritual knowledge and practicing those methods that spiritualize your consciousness. Remember, the point is that the more spiritual become, the more you can recognize, realize and perceive that which is spiritual. The doorway is within you. You merely have to open it. And when that door is opened, the world will look much different, more joyous, happier, and clearer than ever before. The purpose for your own existence will also become more recognizable. You will know what to do and how to function according to that purpose. You will see that being on the spiritual journey is but an exciting adventure that brings you ever higher to newer realizations, opportunities and potentials that you may not have thought of before. And this is what can make all the difference.

THE PRIME REASON FOR SUFFERING

The prime reason for suffering is ignorance. And when we talk of ignorance, we mean ignorance of the soul and our spiritual identity. It is this lack of knowledge and insight which is the basis of our being stuck in the illusion of thinking that our primary identity is the body in which we exist. In that condition, a person becomes overly concerned with the superficial problems of life, such as those that deal with the body and all kinds of bodily relations. This does not mean that one should give up the responsibilities that one has accepted, but that there is another aspect of life that a person in spiritual ignorance will overlook. And that can be resolved through acquiring spiritual knowledge and by attaining the spiritual perspective.

The fact is that the problems of material life are never fully resolved, they come and go like the waves of an ocean. In other words, no matter what you do, what arrangements you make, newer problems are just over the horizon approaching you with every moment that goes by. Such problems of life will keep you absorbed until the day you die, preoccupied with trying to solve your own difficulties and challenges along with those of your family and everyone you are connected with. The best solution is to get out of the ocean, and in this case it means not to simply give it up or walk away from it, but to rise above its troubling effects with spiritual knowledge.

In many cases, we can see that people think that as soon as they have enough money, all their problems will be solved. Though money may help, it cannot provide the ultimate security against the problems of birth, old age, disease, and death. These will never go away and will be waiting for you regardless of how you have arranged your position materially. However, the soul is above such problems and are never touched by them. So, we simply have to reach the spiritual perception to see that such problems are not as big as many people often think they are, and how to rise above the identification of such problems though we may still have to deal with them, but with a less desperate disposition.

Therefore, the real difficulty is being ignorant of our real position as a spiritual being. Such ignorance keeps us bound to material existence, and to the attachment to catering to our body and position as the means to find real happiness. Thus, not only are we compelled to work so hard to make all the arrangements we think will solve our problems, but we also become addicted to various pleasures for this temporary body in our search for happiness. Again and again we go after some means of drifting into a state of pleasure that makes us forget our difficulties, only to again come back to facing the many weaknesses or challenges we have and from which we want to escape. This turns into a vicious cycle, an habitual and repetitive pattern that becomes increasingly difficult from which to be free, until we can see that we are more than this

Ignorance of the Soul

material identity, more than this mind and body that is seeking escape from our difficulties and the circumstances in which we find ourselves. We have to rise above it to be free from it. Otherwise, such addictions for catering to the mind and senses keep us imprisoned to the thought pattern that we are this body that needs the escape we have become accustomed to for relief. This only perpetuates the problem until we change our view of who we are and what we actually need. Thus, it is genuine spiritual knowledge which can point the way for us to understand who we really are and how to see beyond the limitations of the material situation. In other words, once we truly know who we are, then we actually see what we are meant to do.

As it is explained in the *Srimad-Bhagavatam* (2.1.4), persons who are devoid of knowledge of the soul do not inquire in to the real problems of life, because of being too attached to the fallible soldiers like body, wife, children, and the whole material situation [and everything the mind and senses demand of us]. Although sufficiently experienced, they still do not recognize the temporary nature of it all.

In this way, though we have seen how everyone else around us has been forced to give up their body and the material circumstances and attachments through death, we become so preoccupied with life, its ups and downs, joys and sorrows, that we no longer see how time is slowly taking everything away from us. We go on as if nothing will change, or as if there is no end. And we become miserable when unexpected difficulties erupt in our lives, which are bound to happen from the start. Thus, we become lost in this world of illusion.

What is the illusion? It is not that this world does not exist. It certainly does exist, it is real, but for only a temporary duration of time. In the same way, material life is like a dream. Our body and our friends also exist, but it is like a dream that affects us only as long as we do not wake up. The dream we have in the night may be wonderfully pleasant, or it may be a horrible nightmare. In either case, once we wake up and realize our actual position, we then remember that it was merely a temporary dream and we again see who we are and what we are really meant to do. Similarly, once we awake to understanding that we are spiritual beings within the material body, we have a different view of life itself. Thus, we have to point ourselves in the right direction to achieve the real purpose of human existence. As it is explained: "One who is sleeping may see many objects of sense gratification in a dream, but such pleasurable things are merely creations of the mind and are thus ultimately useless. Similarly, the living [spiritual] entity who is asleep to his spiritual identity also sees many objects for pleasing the senses, but these innumerable objects of temporary gratification are creations of the Lord's illusory potency and have no permanent existence. One who meditates upon them [in longing], impelled by the senses, uselessly engages his intelligence." (*Bhag.*11.10.3)

Thus, the material lifestyle is the dream from which we must, sooner or later, awake from. That is why self-realization is also called a spiritual awakening. This spiritual awakening is the revival of our natural spiritual consciousness. If we do not become aware of our spiritual identity, then we can fall ever deeper into material life and further away from spiritual consciousness. As the *Srimad-Bhagavatam* (4.22.31-33) explains: "When one deviates from his original spiritual consciousness, he loses the capacity to remember his previous position [as a spiritual being in a prior existence] or recognize his present one [as a spiritual entity inside a material body]. When remembrance is lost, all knowledge acquired is based on a false foundation [of thinking we are this body]. When this occurs, those learned in spiritual knowledge consider that the soul is lost. There is no stronger obstruction to one's self-interest than thinking other subject matters to be more pleasing or more important than one's self-realization. For human society, constantly thinking of how to earn money and apply it for pleasing the senses brings about the destruction of everyone's real interests. When one becomes devoid of spiritual knowledge and devotional service [or spiritual practice], he enters into lower species of life."

In this way, in material life, one develops a particular kind of consciousness, and that consciousness will take one to the appropriate kind of existence in one's next life that is most suitable for one's level of thinking, feeling and willing. In other words, if a person is focused mostly on things like eating, sleeping, mating, and defending, then that is the ordinary consciousness that we see in most animals. In such a case, how high of a status of life can a person acquire if he has developed only this level of consciousness? Thus, it is the responsibility of any entity who attains human existence to take advantage of it and add the serious pursuit of spiritual knowledge, over and above pious religion, to whatever else he does with this life. Otherwise, he repeats the pattern of material existence time and time again without knowing how to get out of it.

As explained in the ancient texts: "Although the material body is different from the soul, because of the ignorance due to [being absorbed in] material association, one falsely identifies oneself with the superior and inferior bodily conditions. Sometimes a fortunate person is able to give up such mental concoction... An unintelligent man, failing to distinguish himself [as the soul] from material nature, thinks nature [or the temporary world] to be real. By contact with it, he becomes completely bewildered and enters into the cycle of [repeated birth and death in] material existence." (*Srimad-Bhagavatam* 11.22.48, 52)

WRONG ATTACHMENTS

The difficulty in being absorbed in material existence is that the living being then develops attachments that keep him bound to the body and all of its accessories, whether they be habits of actions, addictions, habitual thoughts, items that he accepts as extensions of his body, which may be family and friends, house and home, or his favorite car, guitar, golf clubs, or any other thing through which he becomes accustomed to express himself. So many connections develop that it becomes endless. Often a person reaches a level of attachment to things that he cannot even think of living without these items, or without being surrounded by such conditions and arrangements. The problem is that death takes it all away, at which time he still hankers for the same items again and again. This is what makes the living being bound to material life with no thought of his or her real spiritual identity, or of ever becoming free.

As it is explained in the *Bhagavad-gita* (3.38): "As fire is covered by smoke, as a mirror is covered by dust, or as the embryo is covered by the womb, similarly the living entity [spirit soul] is covered by different degrees of lust." And it is this lust, this desire to attain material conditions and misleading attachments for the temporary happiness and pleasure of the mind and senses that keeps a person blind from either perceiving or even wanting to understand his spiritual identity. It keeps him bound in the wrong direction. Why is it wrong? Because in the end it does not really satisfy him, it does not really fulfill him or make him truly happy. That is why it is said that working so hard for that which is temporary is like working so hard for nothing at all. It is like filling a bowl full of cool water, not knowing that the bowl has a small crack in the bottom. In the beginning it looks so good, so full of promise, but in the end it only offers emptiness, leaving you with nothing.

For this reason it is sometimes very realistically and

Ignorance of the Soul

bluntly related, "This material body is like a house in which I, the soul, am living. The bones forming my spine, ribs, arms and legs are like the beams, crossbeams and pillars of the house, and the whole structure, which is full of stool and urine, is covered by skin, hair and nails. The nine doors leading into this body are constantly excreting foul substances. Besides me, what woman could be so foolish as to devote herself to this material body, thinking that she might find pleasure and love in this contraption?" (*Bhag*.11.8.35)

By meditating on this verse, we can begin to understand that the body is not who we really are, but it is like a foreign dress made by nature to suit the desires of the individual who is meant to wear it, or live in it. But while living in such a vehicle, we have the choice to either act as if we are these bodies, or endeavor to attain spiritual knowledge and realize we are only the living being within the body.

As we move forward through this information, it should become clear that the body is not as important as the soul within it. Without the soul, there is no life. It is the soul that provides life to the body, and is also the motivating factor for one's self-preservation, and our willingness to continue working to preserve and protect this body. This is natural, but we must also be careful not to get overly attached to the bodily concept of life, thinking that this is all that matters. As explained, it is due to the bodily concept of life that the *jiva* soul forgets his real identity as a spiritual being, though he is actually a part of parcel of the Supreme Being. (*Bhag*.8.3.29) As long as the spirit soul is covered by the subtle body, consisting of the mind, intelligence and false ego, he is bound to the results of his fruitive activities [those activities from which he wants to enjoy the outcome]. Because of this covering, the spirit soul is connected with the material energy and must accordingly suffer material conditions and reversals, continually, life after life. (*Bhag*.7.2.47)

This describes how the spirit soul goes through the ups and downs of life because of its connection with the material energy due to being covered by the body. This is a natural course of events, as long as one remains fixed and focused on the material platform. Lord Krishna explains this in the *Bhagavad-gita* (2.14-15), "The nonpermanent appearance of happiness and distress, and their disappearance in due course, are like the appearance and disappearance of winter and summer seasons. They arise from sense perception, and one must learn to tolerate them without being disturbed... The person who is not disturbed by happiness and distress and is steady in both is certainly eligible for liberation."

This means that the more we become fixed on our spiritual identity, the less we will be disturbed by the constant changes that go on around us. Thus, we do not worry about all the variations of life, knowing full well that we are not the drama that we see or experience, but our real identity is on a completely different and higher level of participation. And if we can become steady in this, meaning steadily focused and aware of our spiritual identity, then in such a balanced view, such a person can make continued spiritual advancement to the point of becoming liberated from the materialistic view of life. Such a state is very rare in this society, yet is the ultimate accomplishment of human existence.

Furthermore, as also related above, because the soul is eternal, which is described elsewhere in this book, if the soul does not become free from materialistic or bodily consciousness, then this will continue life after life until the soul is released from this bodily conception. The way the soul becomes entangled in the material energy is described that the living being begins using his material senses to try to enjoy various sense objects that are composed of material nature. Because of this he misidentifies the created material body with the unborn eternal self and becomes entangled in the illusory energy of the Supreme. (*Bhag*.11.3.5) In other words, the person, though a spiritual being, misidentifies his real self with the temporary body, and then works to satisfy the mind, body and senses in so many ways, such as finding beautiful things to see, hear, touch, taste, and so on, while ignoring the needs of the soul. The need of the soul, actually, is complete freedom, freedom from problems, limitations, dept, old age and disease, etc. That is what most people are trying to achieve at present, but through material arrangements, such as ways of trying to keep their youth, attain wealth, avoid disease and stay healthy, remain looking beautiful, etc., which are never completely attainable, nor do such arrangements for the body in this world last for long. Such endeavors are, thus, done in the wrong direction.

The problem with this is that the material universe that we perceive through our mind, eyes, ears, and other senses is an illusory [temporary] creation that one imagines to be real due to the influence of *maya* [the illusory potency]. "In fact, you should know that all of the objects of the material senses are temporary." (*Bhag*.11.7.7) The universe is certainly real, it is here, but it is temporary and always changing. Nothing lasts forever, and sometimes not even for a few years. That is the problem and is the basis of the misidentification of the eternal soul with the impermanent material body, along with all of the wrong attachments and misguided aims of life that develop from that mistaken identification.

THE MISGUIDED AIM OF LIFE

The result of spiritual ignorance and wrong attachments is the misguided aims of life. As explained, it is attraction to the temporary that keeps one focused on bodily conceptions and bodily attachments. It is the desire for gratifying the senses which are the root cause of materialistic existence. And this root desire for happiness and pleasure often evolves around sex, sex as a means of the greatest enjoyment, or sex and the interest in it as the greatest escape from the doldrums of life, or sex as the most necessary way to express love for another person, all of which are misguided aims of life. Why? Because a person can never be fully satisfied through sex, and if love depends on sexual satisfaction, then it is lust and not love, and is then already finished before it even begins because that also never lasts permanently. This basis for love and happiness is completely impermanent. If it is real love, then it must be based on reality, which is spiritual. Love based on the knowledge of the soul will shine on, not burn and then gradually fade out, which is the usual case in material affairs.

Therefore, the bottom line here is that the root cause for our continued material existence in this earthly realm is the desire for, and the endeavor to attain, the gratification of our temporary mind and senses. This can only be changed by learning about and seeing our true spiritual identity. Otherwise, it is like trying to pamper a paper bag that has been placed over our body. We can do so much for the paper bag, rub it nicely, try to feed it tasty foods, give it compliments, but the real person is within. By neglecting the person within, no matter what you do for the bag, the person will still be dissatisfied and in need of the essentials of life. Similarly, no matter what we do for the material body, if we neglect the real person or soul within, he will still be in want or in need of real attention, real love, real freedom. And you cannot be free if you are tied up, enslaved and controlled by the demands of the mind and senses. You cannot be truly free if you are still imprisoned within a temporary material body.

Therefore, in conclusion to this point, we need to understand that working only to fulfill the desires of the mind and body is the root cause of all other misguided aims of life. Thus, the key point to understand here is: Though the individual spirit souls are all parts and parcels of the Supreme Being, it is through His illusory energy, which is unstoppable and difficult to perceive, through which the *jivas* become bewildered by their identifying with various material bodies in which they appear. (*Bhag.*12.6.29)

In this way, it is merely the perception of who and what we think we are that makes the difference. It is through the desire to unnecessarily enjoy the senses, to enjoy the body, that makes one increasingly attached to it, and, thus, prevents one from realizing the self, the real identity that is within yet so much higher than the dull material and temporary physical form. It is by understanding this point that should make clear the foolishness in the materialistic lifestyle. It has been established long ago that everyone must die, at which time we must give up everything that we have accumulated or accomplished that is connected with the material body. And yet, with no level of spiritual realization, most people know nothing about how to make the best situation for themselves in the next life, or how to acquire a spiritual body in the spiritual world, which is eternal, and full of bliss and knowledge. In spite of the fact that this life is only for about 50 to 100 years in duration, most people have made little if any genuine spiritual progress which can be applied for our future existence. Where is the sense in this?

This is why it is explained that though the Supreme Being offers all facility for the conditioned souls, people in general fail to delight in spiritual pursuits and in understanding God. Instead, because they persistently hope for success in their devotion to the unreal and temporary, they continue to wander throughout this fearful world, assuming various degraded material bodies. Thus, they commit spiritual suicide by worshipping and remaining attached to the illusion. (*Bhag*.10.87.22)

ALL SUFFERING EXISTS ONLY WITHIN THE ILLUSION

What many people do not realize is that the body itself, though it seems quite natural for us to inhabit, is the source of any suffering, and being in the illusion is the cause of all misery. There is no suffering in the spiritual reality.

Unfortunately, the common people in this world engage in activities in hopes of enjoying the fruits of their actions. This would seem to be a natural state, but all such actions are almost always for the benefit of the temporary body while ignoring the eternal soul. Thus, in the long run of such a lifestyle, many people find neither true satisfaction nor the mitigation of distress. In fact, sometimes people simply become more aggravated by such activities, meaning that they may think they are solving their problems, but by their foolish decisions their difficulties only increase. (*Bhag*.3.5.2)

Therefore, we need to understand that one who works simply for fruitive activities remains in various degrees of fear because all such actions, results of such actions, and even the purpose of such activities, meaning the body, are subject to end or die. Due to the fact that the body is bound to expire at some point, and that we may lose all of the results for which we have worked, all such actions and the things we have acquired from them become a source of distress and fear as we try to secure and hang on to them for as long as possible. Or they lead to lamentation if we should lose such things, whether they be our possessions or our body, or those we love. But the fact remains, "For one who has taken birth, death is certain, and for one who is dead, birth is certain [into another form somewhere at some time]. Therefore, in the unavoidable discharge of your duty, you should not lament." (*Bg*. 2.27) This is the main pattern of life for which we should be prepared with spiritual knowledge. But what is our main duty? To maintain this body, yes, but more importantly to understand the soul within it. Without that, what have we accomplished when we know that after all that we have done or tried to do, we will only die and later reappear in this creation in some other form again and again, repeatedly?

The next point to understand is that, basically, the sufferings that we undergo are superficial. We are the eternal soul within, but it is the body that interacts with the various material conditions that cause us trouble and distress, while the soul remains aloof or unaffected. Whether our problems are from other living beings, from nature, or from our own body, they are unavoidable. They cannot be stopped while we are in this material world. But we can rise above them by understanding our real identity. And that is a matter of consciousness. Developing the right consciousness is what can decrease the effects of the material conditions that happen around us. As stated: "Whenever a person experiences by self-realization, that both the gross physical and subtle bodies have nothing to do with the pure soul, at that time he sees himself [as the soul within] as well as the Lord." (*Bhag*.1.3.33)

Therefore, the soul is beyond the impermanent troubles that are natural to material existence. The creation itself is temporary, so it is to our best interest to identify with what is eternal. That does not mean that all such problems will stop, but that we will no longer identify with them as effecting our real selves. We may even die, meaning our bodies, but the eternal soul will go on. That is why *Bhagavad-gita* (2.25) relates, "It is said that the soul is invisible, inconceivable, immutable, and unchangeable. Knowing this, you should not grieve for the body."

This is a very important point to understand. No matter what kind of suffering we may feel, whether it is hunger, the need for sleep, our anger, jealously, anxiety, fear of something, it is all based on identifying with our physical or mental well-being. It's all connected with bodily concerns.

If we were really and fully situated in the spiritual aspect of life, we would never feel any suffering. That does not mean that we would not be concerned for those who remain in the illusion of the temporary joys and sorrows of life and feel a need to help them. Naturally, compassion is one of the feelings of the soul, wanting to do good for others who are all parts of God. But for ourselves, once we are spiritually situated, we can see that happiness and distress in material life is built around mental constructs or confusion. (*Bhag.* 11.23.59) It is our material conditioning that makes us feel that one situation is good or pleasant, and something else is bad or unpleasant. Similarly, our creation of friends and enemies in this world is built on this same sort of mental interpretation and conditioning, like a dream wherein we create so many situations out of imagination or impressions from the subconscious. (*Bhag.* 4.9.33) This is the way we interpret through our senses and mind the life we have around us, and what we want to have.

The fact is that we are all spiritual beings, sons and daughters of God. Yet, when we are all acting on the impulse that we are these material bodies which need to be satisfied according to the desires in the mind, it forces us to act in many different selfish ways which are then interpreted as being friendly to some and adverse to others, or wanting one thing and avoiding something else. It is all on the illusory stage of material life, each of us wearing a particular costume, yet whose real identity is far different than the part that we play. The spirit soul naturally exists in a unified state of pure consciousness. However, when appearing in this world and in a variety of forms, each can be overwhelmed and mistaken regarding the purpose of life and our real identity. Thus begins the false conception of life.

Because the material world is an illusion of flickering commodities that are "Here today, gone tomorrow," our numerous attachments tend to be the cause of our anxiety. For example, in thinking that our mortal body is our real self, we become attached to what gives any little pleasure or happiness. Thus, we become attached to our spouses, children, wealth, house, property, or our career. And by trying to hold on to them and keep life balanced so that we can protect all that we have and see that everything flows smoothly, these very attachments put us in a position which creates most of our worry and concern. (*Bhag.* 10.51.47)

In this way, we may begin to see that our position in

Ignorance of the Soul

this world, being a misidentification of what we really are, for the most part, is full of fear, or anxiety, worry, and concern. (*Bhag.* 1.11.3) There may be some happiness, but that also depends on forgetting the concerns that constantly affects us. We must work for our food, our shelter, clothes, our health, our means of transportation, our protection, and so on. Not only do we want to maintain what we have, but we must also continue to provide for our dependents as well.

Furthermore, another basic concern that seems to pervade society is the simple problem of finding a perfect mate. What if a person can't find someone? Will he or she have to live alone? What if she finds someone and he is not what she was hoping for? Then will she have to start all over again? This just goes on and on, for both men and women. When does it end? Or sometimes even if things are going well, we still become afraid of what kind of problem might happen next. We may feel fear that if we lose our job or become unemployed, will we become homeless, or dumped by our spouse, and then worry about the safety of our children, etc. Therefore, in many ways, the happiness we perceive is merely the forgetfulness of the constant problems that this world presents. However, all of these problems exist only within the illusion that we are these temporary bodies. From that misconception comes all of this fear and the sources of anxiety.

Outside of this illusion, within the real understanding of who and what we are, there is no fear, no suffering, and no anxiety. We just need to reach that state of perception. That is why, as it is explained in *Bhagavad-gita* (5.22), a wise person on the spiritual path, or one who knows his real spiritual identity, does not rely on the sources of happiness that come through contact with the material senses because they all have a beginning and an end. This is why when you depend too much on such forms of happiness, these kinds of pleasures can also become sources of misery or disappointment when they are gone, or when you want them and can no longer get them. This is another example of how all suffering exists only within the illusion. That is why it is further explained in the *Srimad-Bhagavatam* (5.5.16) that due to spiritual ignorance, the materialistic person does not know anything about his real self-interest, the auspicious path of life for spiritual advancement. He is simply bound to material enjoyment by lusty desires, and all his plans are for this purpose. Due to this mentality for temporary sense gratification he plunges into the ocean of suffering. Such a foolish person does not even understand how this happens.

Real truth is not material nor temporary. It is the eternal knowledge of the soul and the one Supreme Being. Bringing this information into one's life is the way by which we can mitigate the misconceptions we have about ourselves, and bring us out of the illusion and into that strata of never-ending happiness. Then we can really begin to help others and know what is best to do and how best to be happy. So, if life is meant to be free from all suffering, especially by understanding our spiritual identity, then how do we take the path that will lead us to such realizations? Finding that is the purpose of life.

CHAPTER THREE

The Purpose of Life

The purpose of life is not merely to work in maintaining and satisfying all the needs of the body and mind. Practically speaking, any animal does that much. So, what is the purpose of the human form of life? To find who and what we really are, and what is the Absolute Truth. Not an easy task, really. But one that is possible nonetheless.

To begin with, when one reaches the human stage of life, he or she should ask a few questions. First, who and what am I? What am I supposed to do now? Where did I come from and where am I going? And what is the Supreme Absolute Truth and prime destination or goal of life? It is said that if a human being does not ask these kinds of questions, he has hardly risen above the animal level. And to remain absorbed in the basic animal stage of existence, running after all the materialistic rewards one can accumulate, a person practically has to forget or remain in ignorance of his real spiritual identity.

What this means is that if a person really understood and perceived his spiritual identity, materialistic life would make no sense. He could never be completely content with simply engaging in the pursuit for material happiness. It would be impossible for him to remain satisfied simply living in the material conditions of life. Such a person would be impelled to go deeper into the meaning of this existence and work on attaining the spiritual platform, the spiritual perception. Even just a shallow glimpse of one's spiritual identity, a small taste of genuine spirituality, makes one forever changed. After that, such a person can no longer accept that this world is merely for gratifying the temporary mind and senses. Such engagements leave him empty, hollow, unfulfilled, and wondering if this is all there is to life. And many are those who find themselves feeling this way and do not know why.

Furthermore, by forgetting or remaining ignorant of one's spiritual identity brings the fear of death. If all you know is your body as your identity, then death is the last thing you want to deal with because it would mean the loss of everything you have worked for, everything and everyone you have loved, all that you have attained, and everything with which you have become familiar. And what is more is that death means not knowing where you are going next. No one wants that, even if they say they are not afraid of death. But through spirituality you begin to understand what lies on the other side beyond death, and then you lose your fear of it, and may even become ready for it.

The fact is that the living beings are parts and parcels of the spiritual bliss, the eternal energy of the Supreme. That is why everyone tries to stay forever young, forever happy, avoiding all that is miserable in whatever way they know best. That is the natural constitutional position of the living entities. But without knowing their spiritual identity, they often do not know what to do. Then the desire to be happy becomes transformed into lust for satisfying the mind and body. This material universe is thus created by the Supreme to give the living beings a chance to satisfy these lustful desires. Then, after many years or even many lifetimes of trying to please the body, mind and senses by making so many material arrangements and yet in the end remaining baffled or unsatisfied by such endeavors, the living being will begin to ask why he is still displeased, or unfulfilled after so many experiences, or still longing to find completion. Then he may start to inquire about his real position, purpose and identity.

The Purpose of Life

That is why the beginning of the *Vedanta Sutras* states *athato brahma-jijnyasa*, which means, "Now (in this human form) one should inquire into the Absolute Truth." Do not waste this time only for animal pursuits in eating, sleeping, mating, and defending what you think is yours. You may indeed have to do these things, but try to do them only to the extent that it is necessary. More importantly, you must use your time to inquire into the knowledge of spiritual truth, up to and including the point of becoming liberated, eternally free from the material conditions in which we presently find ourselves. This is the real purpose of life. This is the real opportunity that we should not miss in this material world. It is not a place in which we are stuck forever, but there is a process by which we can free ourselves from this condition of being bound to this material body and this existence. This is what we must learn if we are to attain the real goal of human life.

It is not that this material creation has arisen by chance. It is not a mere coincidence that we are here. Atheists may say that there is no cause or foundation to this creation, and that it is only for enjoying our senses, but that is not the fact. Such people are only spiritually inexperienced and have no knowledge or faith in anything more than what they see or perceive with their material senses. Thus, they have much progress to make before they have any inkling of the real purpose of this life, based on their real spiritual identity of which they remain blind. As it is said in the *Srimad-Bhagavatam* (9.24.58): "The Supreme Personality of Godhead acts through His material energy in the creation, maintenance and annihilation of this cosmic manifestation just to deliver the living entity by His compassion and stop the living entity's [repeated] birth, death and duration of material life. Thus, He enables the living being to return home, back to Godhead."

Therefore, the living beings can cultivate either activities for gratifying the senses, or for attaining ultimate liberation, according to their desire. They have the choice to use this life in whatever way they want. But it is advised that the spiritual process is best for their real well-being. After all, no matter what we do for the body, the real need of the soul is to attain complete freedom from these limitations of being in the body, being in this three-dimensional universe, and to be completely unrestrained in the spiritual domain and in expressing its love toward other spirit souls and the Supreme Spirit. This freedom is never reached while one is misidentifying himself as this temporary material body, or as a product of the cosmic creation, or through the misaligned affection for gross material objects. A person must go much higher than that.

The material world is only a perverted reflection, like a holographic representation of the spiritual world. It is also where the conditioned souls who want to remain separate and independent from God can stay and pretend to be whatever they want to be, starting with being this temporary material body. From there such misidentification expands to thinking one is white, black, American, Russian, rich, poor, fat, skinny, or a member of a certain tribe or society for which he should work against those who are different, or any number of other identities. However, this only deepens the bondage to material existence and makes it all the more difficult to ever understand the spiritual essence within this mask of the body. Only by understanding our spiritual identity can we become free from all such misconceptions.

This is why the *Katha Upanishad* (1.3.3-9) explains that the body is like a chariot with the soul sitting within it. The intellect is the charioteer, and the mind is the reins. The senses are the horses, and the objects that attract the senses are the roads on which the chariot travels. When the soul identifies with the body, senses and mind, he is then considered to be the enjoyer of the actions of these. But he who has no understanding of one's spiritual identity, and whose reins are not firmly held in control, his senses (horses)

The Purpose of Life

are unmanageable, like vicious beasts that take the charioteer in different directions. He thus remains in material existence and goes through the rounds of birth and death. But he who has understanding and whose mind is always firmly held, his senses are under control, like good horses of a charioteer. He remains mindful and pure and reaches that place from where he is not born again, that highest place of Lord Vishnu.

That is why it is also explained that those in the human form who are self-controlled and become expert in spiritual science can directly see the Supreme Being, Lord Krishna, along with all of His potencies. (*Bhag.*11.7.21) This is the potential when using the human form of life to its highest purpose. In this position, a person can reach immortality by entering the spiritual strata through such means. This is why the *Chandogya Upanishad* (8.1.1) relates that out of everything that we may do, within the body is a small lotus, which is the residence of the soul, and that is what is to be sought.

For this reason, a person should work for the ultimate end, the highest accomplishment, not mere fleeting moments of pleasure that may eventually come of its own accord. This is related as follows: "Persons who are actually intelligent and philosophically inclined should endeavor only for that purposeful end which is not obtainable even by wandering from the topmost planet [Brahmaloka] down to the lowest planet [Patala]. As far as happiness derived from sense enjoyment is concerned, it can be obtained automatically in course of time, just as in course of time we obtain miseries even though we do not desire them." (*Bhag.*1.5.18)

Therefore, the ultimate purpose of life is to realign our activities for understanding our spiritual identity, while limiting those actions that would keep us bound to material attachments. That brings us to a higher consciousness by which we can actually perceive our spiritual position. "Thus, clearly understanding by discriminating logic the unique position of the Absolute Truth, one should expertly refute one's misidentification with matter and cut to pieces all doubts about the identity of the self. Becoming satisfied in the soul's natural ecstasy, one should desist from all lusty engagements of the material senses." (*Bhag*.11.28.23) Thus, the real pleasure and happiness we are looking for is within, in the soul's natural ecstasy that is achieved by attaining our normal position as the spiritual being that we are, and in the highest bliss that is attained in connection with the Supreme Spirit.

In fact, the danger of ignoring this duty to attain this insight and perception is outlined herein: "Any person who engages himself within this material world in performing activities that necessitate great struggle, and who, after obtaining a human form of life–which is a chance to attain liberation from all miseries–yet still undertakes the difficult tasks of fruitive activities, must be considered to be cheated and envious of his own soul." (*Bhag*.4.23.28)

Why is a person cheated if he or she does not understand one's spiritual identity? Because he is then forced to again enter another round of birth and death in another material body without having made much progress up the ladder of true development. This is stated in the *Katha Upanishad* (2.6.4) where it simply says that if a man cannot understand this before the falling asunder of his body, then he has to take birth in a material body again in the worlds of creation.

Furthermore, there is no way of knowing exactly what the conditions will be in our next life. It may be nice and pleasant if our activities in this present life are good, or we may find ourselves in difficult or treacherous conditions, according to the dictates of our karma. This is the danger that we face, and for which the risks are hardly worth it if, by our present spiritual pursuits, we can assure ourselves of a better future life, or even the freedom from any future rounds of existence in this world if we can realize the soul's natural bliss and ecstasy by attaining the spiritual realm. The thing to

The Purpose of Life

understand is that this bliss far outweighs the material joys and happiness experienced through sensual delights of the mind and senses. It can be such a degree of ecstasy that it becomes indescribable, and we wonder why it took so long for us to discover it or be convinced that it even existed. This is what the deepest levels of spiritual knowledge recommend for those who are serious about spiritual life, or even those who are slightly inquisitive about our real spiritual identity. This is the true purpose and advantage in utilizing the human body and intellect in such a way. Otherwise we lose this rare opportunity on cheaper and less significant goals. We should meditate on the importance of this as it is described in the following verse:

"The human body, which can award all benefit in life, is automatically obtained by the laws of nature, although it is a very rare achievement. This human body can be compared to a perfectly constructed boat having the spiritual master as the captain and the instructions of the Supreme Being as favorable winds impelling it on its course. Considering all these advantages, a human being who does not utilize his human life to cross the ocean of material existence must be considered the killer of his own soul." (*Bhag*.11.20.17)

Here it is clarified that obtaining the human form of life is a very rare position to attain. One should not treat it lightly, or you may lose a great advantage of being able to escape from material existence and enter into the spiritual realm. The material worlds and the existence therein is compared to an ocean that one can cross by using the body, compared to a boat, to sail across the ocean with the use of the winds of the instructions of a genuine spiritual master and the Supreme Being, as we are presenting in this book. Thus, this verse also outlines one of the first steps in learning how best to engage in spiritual life–approaching a genuine spiritual master for proper guidance.

The *Mundaka Upanishad* confirms this in the verse that says *tad-vijnanartham sa gurum evabhigacchet*: "To understand that transcendental science, one must approach a genuine spiritual master." How to approach such a master is further explained by Lord Krishna in the *Bhagavad-gita* (4.34): "Just try to learn the truth by approaching a spiritual master. Inquire from him submissively and render service unto him. The self-realized soul can impart knowledge unto you because he has seen the truth."

In this way, a genuine spiritual master can give knowledge of the path that one should take and the methods and practices that one should perform for continued and sure spiritual progress. This is the first mentioning of the path to realize our spiritual identity, which we will begin to explain in the next chapter.

CHAPTER FOUR

The Path of Realization

It is described in the *Chandogya Upanishad* (8.7.1-8.12.5) that many thousands of years ago, Lord Brahma, the secondary creator of the universe after the Supreme Lord Vishnu, once explained, "The self which is free from sin, free from old age, from death and grief, from hunger and thirst, which desires nothing but what it ought to desire, and imagines nothing but what it ought to imagine, that is what we must search out, that is what we must try to understand. He who has searched out that self and understands it obtains all worlds and (fulfills) all desires.

At that time both the *devas* (demigods) and *asuras* (demons) both heard these words and agreed that they should search out that self by which one can obtain all worlds and all desires. Thus, Indra from the *devas* and Virochana from the *asuras* both decided to approach Brahma, accepting him as their master. They stayed with Lord Brahma for 32 years as pupils. Thereafter, Brahma finally asked them for what purpose did they stay.

They both replied that after hearing Brahma's statement about the soul, that for he who searched for it and understood it could obtain all worlds and all desires, they both wished to attain that self.

Brahma, beginning with his first and most basic instruction, replied that the person that is seen with the eye, that is the self. This is the immortal, the fearless, this is Brahman.

They asked, "Sir, he who is perceived in the water, and who is perceived in the mirror, who is he?"

Brahma answered, "He himself indeed is seen in all of these. Now look at your self in a pan of water and whatever you do not understand of your self, come and tell me."

They both did so and said that they both see the self, a picture detailed even to the hair and nails.

Brahma then instructed, "After you have cleaned yourselves, adorned yourselves, have put on your best clothes, look again into the water pan. What do you see?"

After doing so, they responded, "We see just as we are, well adorned, with our best clothes, thus we are both there."

Brahma then described, "That is the self, this is the immortal and the fearless, the Brahman."

Then they both went away satisfied in their hearts. But Brahma, looking after them said, "They both go away without having perceived and without having known the self, and whoever of these two, whether *devas* or *asuras*, will follow this doctrine will perish."

Virochana, satisfied in his heart, went to the other *asuras* and preached that doctrine to them, that the self (the body) alone need be worshipped, that the body alone is all that need be served, and that he who worships the self (body) and serves that self, gains both worlds in this and the next life.

Therefore, they call even now a man who does not give alms (to the renunciants), and who has no faith (in spiritual instructions), and offers no worship, is an *asura*, for this is the doctrine of the *asuras*. For even now they deck the body of the dead with perfumes, flowers, and fine raiment by way of ornaments, and think that they will thus conquer the world.

However, Indra, before he had returned to the *devas*, saw a difficulty in the teachings given by Brahma. As this self, as reflected in the water, is well adorned when the body is well adorned, well cleaned if the body is well cleaned, well

The Path of Realization

dressed if the body is well dressed, that same self will be blind if the body is blind, lame if the body is lame, crippled if the body is crippled, and will perish in fact as soon as the body perishes. "Therefore," Indra explained, "I see no good in this doctrine."

Then taking fuel in hand as an offering, he again approached Lord Brahma. Then Lord Brahma said, "Indra, you went away with Virochana, satisfied in your heart, for what purpose did you come back?"

Indra replied, as this self, when reflected in the water, is well adorned when the body is well adorned, well cleaned if the body is well cleaned, well dressed if the body is well dressed, that same self will be blind if the body is blind, lame if the body is lame, crippled if the body is crippled, and will perish in fact as soon as the body perishes. "Therefore, I see no good in this doctrine."

"So, it is indeed, Maghavat (Indra)," replied Lord Brahma. "But I shall explain to you the nature of the true self. Live with me another 32 years."

Thus, Indra lived with Brahma for another 32 years, after which Brahma explained that he who moves about [in a subtle form, free from the gross material body], happy in dreams, that is the immortal, the fearless, this is Brahman."

Then again Indra went away satisfied in his heart. But then again he saw some difficulty in this doctrine. Although it is true that self is not blinded, even if the body is blind, nor lame if the body is lame, nor rendered faulty by the faults of the body. Still, if in dreams someone strikes him, chases him, he is still conscious of pain and suffering. Therefore, where is the good in this doctrine?

So, again Indra went back to Brahma and complained of these faults in this doctrine. And again Brahma asked him to live with him as a pupil for 32 years. Thereafter, Brahma explained that when a man being asleep, reposing and at perfect rest, sees no dreams, that is the self, this is the immortal, the fearless, that is Brahman. Then Indra went away satisfied in heart. But again while he was leaving he could understand that actually he does know what is the self, or what is anything. Thus, he is still going toward utter annihilation. There is no good in this.

Again, Indra, with fuel in hand approached Lord Brahma and explained his difficulty. Brahma replied, "So it is indeed, Maghavat, but I shall explain to you the true self and nothing more. Live here another five years."

So, Indra lived as a pupil in Brahma's care for another five years, which completed 101 years. Thereafter, Brahma spoke to Indra, "This body is mortal and always held by death. It is the abode of the real self which is immortal and without a body. When in the body, that self is held by pleasure and pain [when thinking this body is the self and the self is the body]. So long as the self is in the body, he cannot get free from pleasure and pain. But when he is free of the body [when he knows the self is different from the physical form, or free from bodily consciousness], then neither pleasure nor pain touches him. The wind is without body, the cloud, lightning, and thunder are without a body. The self also, arising and free from this body, appears in its own form, as soon as it has approached the highest light [the spiritual knowledge of the Supreme]. The soul, in that state, moves about laughing, playing and rejoicing, no more minding that body into which he was born."

Thus, the *devas* who are in the world of Brahman meditate on that self (as taught by Brahma and by Indra to the *devas*). Therefore, all worlds and all desires belong to them. He who knows that self and understands it, obtains all worlds and all desires.

The significance of this story is that there are different levels of realizations, from the physical, mental, intellectual, the dream world, to the spiritual world of the soul. Furthermore, it shows that genuine spiritual understanding is very difficult to find, and one must be serious to attain such rare knowledge if he or she is going to make actual spiritual progress and attain the perception of the soul. Otherwise, it is something that is easy to talk about, for even a child of eight years old may know of this, but hardly a man of eighty can actually perceive it. Thus, one must remain steady and determined to reach that state of spiritual perception, self-realization. That is what separates the men from the boys, so to speak.

Thus, the ultimate purpose of the path of religion is not for material blessings, even though they may be included. But it is to adopt the practice of those methods that will release oneself from bondage to this material body and its consequential existence and regain the life of freedom in the spiritual world, the natural home and blissful state of being for the eternal soul. How this is accomplished is described as follows:

"If the [effect of the] illusory energy [*maya*] subsides and the living entity becomes fully enriched with [spiritual] knowledge by the grace of the Lord, then he becomes at once enlightened with self-realization and then situated in his own glory." (*Srimad-Bhagavatam* 1.3.34) This is what it takes to become free from thinking that you are no more than your limited material body, but to know that you are the unlimited spirit soul within it. This also means that the appearance of the soul's material existence is actually false. The soul, due to false ego, may identify with the body, but the soul itself actually does not come in contact with the material arrangements that go on around it, but only seems to experience it through the attachment to the body. This is well known and more fully explained in the ancient text of *Srimad-Bhagavatam* (11.23.50-55) as it says:

"If you say that these people [around me] are the cause of my happiness and distress, then where is the place of the soul in such a conception? This happiness and distress pertain not to the soul but to the interactions of material bodies. If someone bites his tongue with his own teeth, at whom can he become angry in his suffering? If you say that the demigods who rule the bodily senses cause suffering, still, how can such suffering apply to the spiritual soul? This acting and being acted upon are merely interactions of the changeable senses... And if we examine the hypothesis that the planets [as astrological influences] are the immediate cause of suffering and happiness, then also where is the relationship with the soul, who is eternal? After all, the effect of the planets applies only to things that have taken birth. Expert astrologers have moreover explained how the planets are only causing pain to each other. Therefore, since the living entity is distinct from these planets and from the material body, against whom should he vent his anger? If we assume that fruitive work is the cause of happiness and distress, we still are not dealing with the soul. The idea of material work arises when there is an actor, the spiritual being, who is conscious, and a material body that undergoes the transformation of happiness and distress as a reaction to such work. Since the body has no life on its own [without the inhabiting soul], it cannot be the actual cause or recipient of happiness and distress, nor can the soul, who is ultimately completely spiritual and aloof from the material body... As fire does not burn its own flames, nor does the cold harm its own snowflakes, the spirit soul is also transcendental and beyond the experience of material happiness and distress."

In conclusion then to this analysis, the soul is beyond the ups and downs, the happiness and distress of material existence. We merely have to regain our identity as the spiritual being to attain that state of being.

Ultimately, it is the mind alone that causes happiness and distress by interpreting things around us as being wanted or unwanted, good or bad, tasteful or distasteful, and, thus, perpetuates material life in this way. (*Bhag.*11.23.42) This is also explained in a different way, that it is the false ego, or the ego of the body, which gives shape to illusory material existence and, thus, experiences material happiness and

The Path of Realization

distress. The spirit soul, however, is transcendental to material nature; he can never actually be affected by material happiness and distress in any place, under any circumstance, or by the agency of any person. A person who understands this has nothing whatsoever to fear from the material creation. (*Bhag.*11.23.56)

We should explain here that everyone has an ego. There is the false ego, which is the idea that we are this body. The false ego makes one think that he or she is a material body of a certain kind, a certain race, or size, or creed, or culture, or even a certain sex. The problem with this is that this identification is temporary. Even if we have a particular name, we may later change it. So, everything connected to this body is subject to change, which means the ego of the body is false or temporary and, thus, misleading. Then there is also the real ego of the soul, which is simply "I am," or "I am spirit." This ego is real because it deals only with the soul, it does not extend to the body and all of the bodily connections. That is the difference between the real ego and the false ego, the latter of which will mislead us into the wrong direction and purpose of life.

In this way, no other force besides one's own mental confusion makes the living being experience happiness and distress. As stated, one's perception of friends, neutral parties and enemies and the whole material life that is built around this concept is simply created out of [spiritual] ignorance. (*Bhag.*11.23.59) In this way, what makes one a friend is mostly mutual behavior. It is similar interests and motivations that often are all that make a friendship. Once those interests or the mutual behavior changes, the friendship also often dissolves. This is how you can tell when the connection is based mostly on ego, or bodily identification and mutual causes.

We have to be able to recognize ourselves more deeply than this. This is what has to be adjusted through spiritual practice. This is why it is further explained that the false ego has no factual basis, yet it is perceived in many ways, such as the functions and attachments of the mind, in style of speech or language, and bodily activities and mannerisms. But with the sword of transcendental knowledge, sharpened by the worship of a genuine spiritual master, a sober sage will cut off this false identification and live in this world free from all material attachment. (*Bhag*.11.28.17)

Of course, a person may not be able to do this overnight, it takes time, education and practice. But this is why spiritual practice must be done with patience and determination. You must simply keep at it in a steady manner, and in time your practice will have so many effects. In time a person will be able to see how it is benefitting him. He will begin to perceive his spiritual identity that is beyond the limitations and influence of the body, and how he can be free from identifying only with material existence. One who is trained in proper spiritual knowledge can see all of this, while others cannot though they may try.

Training is a key point here because it takes an adjustment of consciousness to be able to perceive the spiritual strata. As related in the *Bhagavad-gita* (13.16): "The Supreme Truth exists both internally [within us] and externally [around us], in the moving and nonmoving. He is beyond the power of the material senses to see or to know. Although far, far away, He is also near to all." Thus, we must go beyond the capacity of the mind and senses to be able to perceive this Supreme Truth. This reverts back to a point that was made regarding becoming free from the control of the senses. The more we are controlled or motivated by the demands of the senses, the longer and more difficult it will be to rise above them and reach the means to perceive that which is spiritual. This is also a direct instruction noted in the *Bhagavad-gita* (3.34): "Attraction and repulsion for sense objects are felt by embodied beings, but one should not fall under the control of the senses and sense objects because they are stumbling blocks on the path of self-realization."

THE SUPREME OCCUPATION AND HIGHEST BLISS

So, what is the best process for accomplishing this goal of self-realization? This is also described as, "The supreme occupation [*dharma*] for all of humanity is that by which men can attain to loving devotional service unto the transcendent Lord. Such devotional service must be unmotivated and uninterrupted to completely satisfy the self." (*Bhag*.1.2.6)

This is the key. The whole process is to eventually regain the natural condition of the soul to engage in serving with love the Supreme Being. The need is to be trained so that such service can go on in a steady and unmotivated fashion, or in a way in which it is not being performed for material rewards. Material rewards means that we only do something for payment, and without the payment, we give it up. So, in the art of spiritual service to God, we must go beyond that. The blessings will naturally be there, but when we can reach this level of engagement that does not depend on material rewards, the soul will be completely satisfied. Why? Because it is the natural, spontaneous condition of the soul that simply needs to be reawakened.

We need to understand that the disposition of the soul is to love and be loved. That is why we are always looking for love in this material existence. It is natural to the soul. But material love of the body, though a reflection of the needs of the soul, is not always fulfilling here because it is not directly connected with the soul. It is based on bodily and mental needs and expressions. So, it misses the real point of what love should be. Why? Because the soul really longs to have spiritual relationships, the topmost being with the Supreme Soul, the ultimate object of our affection. When we have a relationship with the Complete, then we feel complete, we are complete. We feel the joy, bliss and fulfillment that we have always wanted to feel that cannot be attained in any other way. This is the nature of the soul, and until we fulfill the needs of the soul in this way, we remain in various levels of being in want, unfulfilled and still looking for meaning, and a way to feel complete. This is the secret. But when we awaken the real nature of the soul as our spiritual identity, and in relation with the Supreme Soul, we can taste a bliss that knows no bounds.

Such inner satisfaction, therefore, is outside or beyond the realm of outer material happiness and pleasure. It is a state of contentment and being satisfied inwardly in whichever condition one finds him or herself through the attainment of inner bliss and happiness. Material sense gratification, on the other hand, leads to the highs and lows of life, in which the mind and senses want a continuous flow of higher highs and more intense thrills. Thus, various addictions arise to get this kind of constant excitement or intoxication. This can also lead simply to the desire for an escape from the difficulties of life, which often brings one to deeper levels of distress and sorrow rather than higher states of happiness. So, this should be avoided by engaging in the means that will simply and most effectively satisfy the soul itself, rather than merely the body that covers it.

The point is that being in spiritual consciousness does not mean that one is blissed-out to the point of being ineffective or dysfunctional. It means simply that one remains steady in spiritual consciousness throughout all conditions of life. "A person who neither rejoices upon achieving something pleasant nor laments upon achieving something unpleasant, who is self-intelligent, unbewildered, and who knows the science of God, is to be understood as already situated in Transcendence." (*Bg*.5.20) This is the main point of being spiritual, that one is steady and equipoised by being focused on one's spiritual identity and connection with the Supreme. The more one lives in this way, the more self-realized and spiritually aware he or she will become. Then the taste and satisfaction that one feels within, connected to the soul, will increase. As it increases, a person will continually live in such consciousness more and more, to the point that, though he may engage in all kinds of activities, inwardly he is never outside of this spiritual perception and natural bliss and happiness. And as one progresses in this way, that bliss can become ecstasy in one's meditation on the soul and Supersoul. This is what we all are ultimately looking for.

The *Taittiriya Upanishad* (2.8.1-5) relates that the highest bliss, higher than all others, is that which comes from understanding the self, the soul. He who knows this bliss fears nothing, and does not distress himself over small concerns, for he has freed himself by such knowledge that leads to that bliss.

The *Chandogya Upanishad* (7.23.1) verifies this, that it is the Infinite that is bliss. There is no bliss in anything finite. Infinity only is bliss. This Infinity, however, is what we must desire to understand.

This goes back to what I said in the previous chapter, that suffering and distress exist only in the illusion, the finite, the material existence, while bliss and ecstasy exist in reality, the spiritual dimension, the infinity. It is the normal situation of the living being, the soul, to be fully satisfied in spiritual bliss. This is the need of the soul, to be completely free, free from the limitations of material existence, free from the constraints of the finite. We are normally happy and blissful when established in spiritual consciousness, in the spiritual strata, and in Infinity. That is why so many people seek such happiness while living in the material body, though they are not always aware of why. Why do people seek to be beautiful, to be young, rich and free to do as they please, and free from all miseries of life? Because that is a reflection of the constitutional position of the soul, which is who and what they really are. That is their normal condition, their normal situation, and is why they try so hard to attain it, if only through bodily or materialistic arrangements, which, unfortunately, are all temporary. Therefore, the living beings need to be trained up properly so they know how to reach the real way to attain the perception of their real spiritual identity. This is the path of realization. Then whatever arrangements they make is not merely for the temporary body, but is in connection with their real identity as the spirit soul.

So, how do we reach this perception? The path is straight and narrow, but does offer some latitude in the means and methods by which we can get there. This is explained on a basic level in the *Bhagavad-gita* (18.51-54): "Being purified by his intelligence [the cultivation of spiritual knowledge] and controlling the mind with determination, giving up [attachment to] the objects of sense gratification, being freed from attachment and hatred, one who lives in a secluded place [meaning to keep materialistic association to a minimum], who eats little and controls the body and the tongue, and is always in trance [or thoughts of the spiritual world and the Supreme Being] and is detached [from sensual and bodily demands], who is without false ego, false strength, false pride, lust, anger, and who does not accept material things, such a person is certainly elevated to the position of self-realization. One who is thus transcendentally situated at once realizes the Supreme Brahman. He never laments nor desires to have anything; he is equally disposed to every living entity. In that state he attains pure devotional service [the natural activity of the soul] unto the Lord."

Of course, this book is only an introduction into the means, ways and methods to spiritualize our consciousness so that we can begin to perceive our real identity as a spiritual being, the soul within. But this information is provided in greater depth in my other books, continuing with "*The Secret Teachings of the Vedas*" and going on to "*The Heart of Hinduism: The Eastern Path to Freedom, Empowerment and Illumination*," and so on. But this should begin to show the potential of what you really are as a spiritual being and how to get started.

Nonetheless, clear information in such texts as the

The Path of Realization

Bhagavad-gita (2.50) continues to show us the means for spiritualizing our consciousness to perceive our spiritual identity, where it says: "A man engaged in devotional service [bhakti yoga] rids himself of both good and bad actions [or good and bad karma] even in this life. Therefore, strive for yoga, which is the art of all work."

This verifies the fact that being engaged in yoga for spiritual progress can free us of all kinds of unwanted factors that can keep us bound to material existence and limitations in our spiritual perception. Bhakti yoga is the devotional form of yoga wherein one dovetails all of one's ordinary activities into spiritual actions for the pleasure of the Supreme. Thus, it is not necessary to remain fixed in quiet or silent meditation to achieve yogic trance, but one can engage in our regular acts while absorbed in spiritual thoughts and consciousness and still attain great strides in spiritual development and see and act as our real identity of the soul.

This is also why bhakti yoga is considered by Lord Krishna Himself as one of the most direct means of spiritual development. Why? Because it directly engages the soul in acts of spiritual activities, which are also intimately connected with the Supreme Being. Bhakti means devotion or love, and as everyone knows, love can be an easy cause for thinking of someone and being absorbed in activities that can support that love. Therefore, Lord Krishna explains in the *Bhagavad-gita* (6.47), "And of all yogis, he who always abides in Me with great faith, worshiping Me in transcendental loving service, is most intimately united with Me in yoga and is the highest of all." In this way, other yogas have particular goals to accomplish for one's development, whether it is karma yoga, hatha yoga, jnana yoga, dhyana yoga, raja yoga, etc. But bhakti yoga brings one very quickly into a relationship with the Supreme Soul, or God, by activating the identity of the living being as a part and parcel of God, an individual soul, the reality within the temporary material body. Thus, no process works more quickly as this method. It is only by one's great good fortune that a person can come to this level of understanding.

* * *

So, in conclusion, what is the ultimate truth that should be understood? "The answer is that nondual [absolute spiritual] knowledge is the ultimate truth. It is devoid of the contamination of material qualities. It gives us liberation [from material existence]. It is the one without a second, all-pervading and beyond imagination. The first realization of that knowledge is Brahman [the eternal atmosphere and great effulgence of spiritual energy, of which the soul is an eternal part]. Then the Paramatma, the Supersoul [in the heart of every living being], is realized by the yogis who try to see Him without grievance. This is the second stage of realization. Finally, full realization of the same supreme knowledge is realized as the Supreme Person [or Bhagavan the Personality of God]. All learned scholars describe the Supreme Person as Vasudeva [also known as Krishna], the cause of the Brahman, Paramatma and others." (*Srimad-Bhagavatam* 5.12.11)

In other words, genuine spiritual realization comes when a person understands the nature of the soul and all three aspects of God. Thus, the essential realization is of our natural spiritual identity as a spirit soul. Then the first aspect of God to understand is the great effulgent Brahman, the expanding white light that is said to be the bodily rays of God. Then the second realization is that of the Supersoul, the localized expansion of God in everyone's heart which accompanies the individual soul in all conditions, and in all types of bodies. Then the final level of realization is to understand the Supreme Personality and form of God, from which all other expansions emanate, such as the *atmas* or souls, the Brahman, Paramatma, and all other *avatars* or expansions of God. From this level of realization we can learn and hear about the many pastimes, activities, characteristics, and personality of that Supreme Being.

Therefore, as the *Chandogya Upanishad* (8.25.2) explains, "For a person who sees, perceives, and understands this spiritual truth, he loves the self, delights in the self and revels and rejoices in the self. Thus, he is master in all the worlds." In other words, he has all that he needs wherever he goes, and has attained the prime goal of human existence. "But those who think differently from this [who think the material body is their real identity], live in perishable worlds, and have other beings for their rulers." This means that it is only a matter of consciousness. If one has a spiritual consciousness and perceives life in that way, he is already a part of the spiritual world. He has recognized who and what he really is, and his connection with the Supreme. However, those who think they are but these material bodies and nothing more, and motivated in that way, are said to live in temporary bodies, ephemeral worlds, and ruled by other material beings. This is not the basis of spiritual reality. Therefore, when they leave their body at death, they cannot go higher than to another material birth, whether in heaven, hell, or the earthly domain to continue to work out their material desires based on their karma and consciousness.

That is why, as verified in the *Katha Upanishad* (2.6.7-9), a person who understands this highest truth, as explained above, becomes liberated from material existence.

CHAPTER FIVE

How the Soul is Eternal

As we make progress on the path to spiritual perception, we begin to actually perceive what the soul is, as it is described in particular ancient texts. As we pointed out earlier, so many religions and cultures throughout the world instruct us on the need and the reason to understand that we are more than this material body, but few of them really describe what the soul is, where it is located, and exactly how to perceive it, and, further, what is the relationship between the soul and God, the Supreme Soul. However, in my personal research, I have found that such information is indeed available, you just have to look in the right place. And that place is in the Vedic texts, which provide more information about this than anywhere else.

Therein we find many kinds of descriptions for the soul, first of which let us know that the soul is eternal. To find some of the quotes that describe this, we can begin with the *Bhagavad-gita* (2.12) wherein Lord Krishna explains to His friend and devotee Arjuna that never was there a time when He did not exist, nor you, nor any of the kings that were there on the battlefield of Kurukshetra, nor in the future shall any of us cease to be.

In this way, we can begin to see that the soul has been around and circulating through situations for eons, countless years, and regardless of what happens to us on the material field of activity, the soul will continue its existence. It is completely separate from the body and whatever happens to

How the Soul is Eternal

this material form in which we temporarily exist. As described: "The soul can never be cut into pieces by any weapon, nor can he be burned by fire, nor moistened by water, nor withered by the wind." (*Bg*.2.23)

"Know that which pervades the entire body [by consciousness] is indestructible. No one is able to destroy the imperishable soul." (*Bg*.2.17)

"One who thinks himself either the cause of destruction or that which is subject to destruction is ignorant of his true self. The soul is beyond such cause and effect." (*Katha Upanishad* 1.2.19)

Thus, the soul cannot be killed or undergo the same reactions that the body does. The body may take birth, undergo so many actions and consequences, and then later die, but the soul is completely transcendental to it all. Actually, the correct view is that "we" are completely transcendental to the body. We should not talk about the soul as if it is some detached object separate from us, for the soul is what we really are, it is *our* real identity, and *we* are eternal. We simply have to realize and perceive who we really are. As further described in the *Srimad-Bhagavatam*:

"The spiritual soul, the living entity, has no death, for he is eternal and inexhaustible. Being free from material contamination, he can go anywhere in the material or spiritual worlds. He is fully aware and completely different from the material body, but because of being misled by misuse of his slight independence, he is obliged to accept subtle and gross bodies created by the material energy and thus be subjected to so-called material happiness and distress. Therefore, no one should lament for the passing of the spirit soul from the body." (*Bhag*.7.2.22)

This clearly points out that once we are free from identifying with the material body as if it is our real identity, we can, once purified in this way, practically go anywhere we want in either the material or spiritual worlds. Such realization is a lofty qualification, but it is also the ultimate goal of real human existence. It is only by being mislead into thinking that the happiness of the body, mind and senses is the main goal in life that we become conditioned to accept this as our normal state of being. Then we are forced to accept life in various subtle and gross bodies that are but different forms and combinations of the material energy and elements, and, thus, we undergo different states of being, which our mind interprets as either happy, sad, good, bad, smooth or distressful. But such changes are typical of material existence. Therefore, we need to free ourselves from such a state and attain spiritual realization, as is further described:

"The soul within the body is self-luminous and is separate from the visible gross body and invisible subtle body [consisting of mind, intelligence and false ego]. The soul remains as the fixed basis of changing bodily existence, just as the sky is the unchanging background of material transformation. Therefore, the soul is endless and without material comparison." (*Bhag*.12.5.8)

Here it is described how the soul is the foundation of everything else regarding our changing existence in this material world. Bodily existence is ever shifting, but the soul does not change. It remains as it is in all circumstances, just like the sky or air remains the same regardless of how everything else in it transforms into different shapes and usages. In this way, we can begin to understand how the soul has no end and cannot be compared to anything in this material realm. It is, and we are, beyond it all.

Now take a moment and try to see yourself in this light. See that you have been the witness in all that you do, all that you have done, for all the years of this life. Maybe it has been good, maybe some of it has been bad or disappointing, but you are still watching what happens to you in this life, in relation to your body. It is almost like watching a movie, your own movie as you grow, develop, mature, learn, and go through life. Yet, inside, you are still the same person. You are the witness of what happens in your life, which also

How the Soul is Eternal

means that in spite of what happens to you or around you, you are, in the ultimate sense, still separate from what happens to the body. This is like the previous example of being the driver in your car. Or, as explained as follows: "One who observes the birth of a tree from its seed, and the ultimate death of the tree after maturity, certainly remains a distinct observer separate from the tree. In the same way, the witness of the birth and death of the material body remains separate from it." (*Bhag.*11.22.50) In other words, the soul, what you are, is in the body but is still different from it because it is spiritual, like a separate element within the body.

In a similar way, we can understand that the soul is eternal, which is because it is a part of the spiritual energy just as the Supreme Being is eternal. The Supreme, however, is the cause and source of the spiritual energy. The soul is but the energy of God, and is, thus, but a part and parcel of God. This is further established as follows: "The same *jiva* [individual soul] is eternal and is for eternity and without a beginning joined to the Supreme Lord by the tie of an eternal kinship. He [the soul] is transcendental spiritual potency." (*Brahma-samhita*, text 21)

The point here is that not only are we eternal, but we are also eternally related with the Supreme Being in a kinship, being of the same eternal nature and potency. The difference is that God is great, we are small. The Supreme is the Infinite, we are infinitesimal, but at the same time eternally related. Nothing can change that, and no religion or institution should try to convince us otherwise, that without the church or institution we have no relationship with God. Nothing can be further from the truth. The only thing that needs to be done is to simply reawaken that relationship. And that is why in the Vedic system there are so many tools or means to help a person do that, whether they be gurus, spiritual teachers, the Vedic texts, the mantras, yoga systems, temples, rituals of worship, etc. They are all for helping us elevate our consciousness to see who and what we really are and what is our eternal relationship with God. It is all based on compassion and unconditional love by which we can again find out who we really are. Everything is meant to help point the way. We merely need to take the lessons of life in the way it can lead us to a higher understanding of who we are on the spiritual level, beyond the body and all its limitations within this three dimensional realm of material existence.

Another way of looking at this is that, "The body indeed withers and dies when the self has left it, but the self does not die. The Supreme Being who is the fundamental cause of this whole world, is eternally existing with His supra-logical power, and thou art that." (*Chandogya Upanishad* 6.11.3) This means that the soul never dies because it is a part of the supreme transcendental energy of God. So, it belongs in and is a part of the spiritual realm, which is also beyond the means of logical understanding. Materialists try to use mundane and ordinary logic to understand God and His supreme spiritual energy, but such logic becomes a subtle trap that confines them to a platform where all things spiritual remain outside their grasp of comprehension. No one can understand the spiritual realm until one can begin to enter into it by raising their consciousness or spiritualizing their awareness. Until then, they are like little children trying to comprehend the world of sophisticated adults. They and their misleading ideas are but sources of amusement for those who are spiritually experienced.

In this way, we also need to understand that the material body is but a temporary vehicle. We must not be overly attached to it. It is not meant to last for long. It has no long term existence of itself, as is the case for all that is part of the material energy. Everything that is part of the material realm goes through six types of changes, such as birth, growth, staying for some time, producing some by-products, then aging or dwindling, and then finally death. Thus, death of the material body is but part of the natural progression of what happens in this material realm, as is also pointed out as follows: "Only the material body of the indestructible, immeasurable and eternal living entity is subject to destruction... For the soul there is never birth nor death. Nor having once been, does he ever cease to be. He is unborn, eternal, ever-existing, undying and primeval. He is not slain when the body is slain." (*Bg*.2.18, 20)

Furthermore, "As the embodied soul continually passes, in this body, from boyhood to youth to old age, the soul similarly passes into another body at death. The self-realized soul is not bewildered by such a change." (*Bg*.2.13) Thus, it is the mission in human life to become self-realized by which we can perceive that which is spiritual, beginning with our own identity is a spiritual being. Then we can perceive the reality of this pattern of life, as described: "As a person puts on new garments, giving up the old ones, similarly, the soul accepts new material bodies, giving up the old and useless ones." (*Bg*.2.22)

Therefore, as it is said, "A person [the soul] does not actually take birth out of the seed of past activities, nor, being immortal, does he die. By illusion the living being appears to be born and to die, just as fire in connection with firewood appears to begin and then cease to exist." (*Bhag*.11.22.46) This makes it obvious, that just as fire is a natural element, it may look like one fire from a particular piece of wood has a beginning and end, as if it is different from another fire, but actually it is the same element regardless of where it appears. It may end with one piece of wood, but it is always existing somewhere. Similarly, the soul may appear to be existing in one body, in one life, and it may seem like it ceases to exist when that body dies, but actually it goes on to appear in another form, another material body. Thus, death of the soul is but an illusion brought on only by appearances in this material realm. And these appearances are often only judgements and interpretations of the mind, which has been conditioned to accept things by its association with other material objects and situations, as it is further explained: "Although the material body is different from the self, because of ignorance due to material association one falsely identifies oneself with the superior and inferior [good or bad] bodily conditions. Sometimes a fortunate person is able to give up such mental concoction." (*Bhag.*11.22.48)

One travels through the different levels of material existence, motivated or impelled by the mind. According to the way the senses perceive the material energy and the way the mind interprets it, we go through different levels of material life, various bodies and identities, moods and dispositions. While actually it is merely differing combinations of the same material elements and energies that come together, then disperse and make another arrangement, which is again interpreted differently by the mind to be either good, bad, happy or sad, and on and on indefinitely until we are finally free from it all. And such freedom is attained by rising above it, transcending it by raising our consciousness with spiritual knowledge at first, and then spiritual practice to heighten our awareness in order to directly perceive the transcendental strata.

The next step is to realize our actual position as spiritual beings within this material body, and, thus, become free from the mental fabrication of our identity as material bodies. We are in this body, and the body is real, but it is temporary, which we will see one way or another, either by self-realization, or with death. But, as it has been related, the self-realized person is not bewildered by such a change. Instead, such a person can utilize death to his or her best advantage, as an opportunity to reach a higher perception of who he or she is as a spiritual and eternal being.

SEEING THE BIG PICTURE

Now, with this knowledge, we should be able to look within ourselves and, even if we cannot yet see it, we should at least get a sense of the timelessness of our real identity, that we have not been born only to die and then drift into nothingness. That is why so many people strive to live a long life, because life is natural and death is not, at least not for the soul. But for the body, death is part of the natural course of events. It is only the end of the body that creates the appearance of birth and death of the person. Yet, the soul goes on. As it is further explained:

"The soul's material life, his experience of sense gratification, is actually false, just like a tree's appearance of quivering when the tree is reflected in agitated water, or like the earth's appearance of spinning due to one's spinning his eyes around, or like the world of a fantasy or dream. For one who is thinking of gratifying the senses, material life, although lacking factual existence, does not go away, just like the unpleasant experiences of a dream [that continues as long as one does not awaken from the dream]." (*Bhag*.11.22.54-56)

In this way, we can begin to understand that it is only from our misleading material perception with our faulty senses that we seem to have an existence that actually affects who and what we are as the soul within. But, as previously related, the soul does not undergo the same kinds of ups and downs as the body. We are actually free of that, but we have to realize and perceive our spiritual identity to attain that freedom. That realization of who and what we really are is the awakening from the dream that we presently experience while we think we are nothing more than this body. The dream may be heavenly or hellish, but we will be affected by it only as long as we are not awakened from it. Yes, we actually had the dream, but when we awaken we know it was temporary, and we realize again who we are and what is our actual position.

In the same way, once we realize our spiritual identity as a timeless being, we become detached from all the things that were once so important to us, that were once such an influence on us in our temporary materialistic lives. That is the rare freedom to be attained in this human existence while we have the intellectual faculties to do so. So, what are we waiting for?

CHAPTER SIX

The Size and Nature of the Soul

When it comes to actually perceiving the soul, not only do we learn that the soul is eternal, but it also has a certain size and location within the physical body, and a particular disposition. To begin with, as it is described in various ancient texts, we can understand that: "The individual *jiva* soul is to be known as subtle, and the size of a hair cut into one hundred parts, and each part cut into a hundred more parts. Yet, he is understood to be qualitatively the same as the Infinite." (*Svetasvatara Upanishad* 5.9)

This describes the subatomic size of the soul. Thus, a hair is generally three-thousandths of an inch in diameter. So, you take a tip of a hair and divide that into one hundred parts, and then one of those parts into another hundred parts, and you have the size of the individual soul. But more than that, it is also spiritual, thus making it even more difficult to perceive by the material senses.

Furthermore, it resides within the company of the Supersoul, both of which reside in the heart of the living being: "That self abides in the heart..." (*Chandogya Upanishad* 8.3.3)

"Now that serene being which, after having risen from out of this earthly body, and having reached the highest light (of spiritual knowledge), appears in its true form, that is the self... This is the immortal, the fearless, this is Brahman [the spiritual essence]. And of that Brahman the name is *Satyam*, Truth." (*Chandogya Upanishad* 8.3.4)

This begins to explain not only the location of the soul in the body of the living being, but also the eternal nature and how it can be seen, which is by realization through transcendental knowledge. It is seen by information received through the ears, by which a person can take to the spiritual practices which purifies or spiritualizes the consciousness so that he or she can actually see the soul as one's true identity. That is the Satyam or Truth of who and what we are.

This is why it is further explained, "That self is hidden in all beings and does not shine forth, but it is seen by subtle seers through their sharp and subtle intellect." (*Katha Upanishad* 1.3.12) Thus, it is through the intellect that one begins to see the truth of who and what we are.

The status of the soul is that it is the most subtle of all elements. "The working senses are superior to dull matter; mind is higher than the senses; intelligence is still higher than the mind; and he [the soul] is even higher than the intelligence. Thus, knowing oneself to be transcendental to material senses, mind and intelligence, one should control the lower self [mind, intelligence and false ego] by the higher self, and thus–by spiritual strength–conquer the insatiable enemy known as lust." (*Bg*.3.42-43) This indicates the refined nature of the soul, and why it cannot be so easily observed by ordinary sensual detection. This is similarly confirmed in other places, such as in the *Katha Upanishad* (1.3.10), which reveals further, "The subtle elements are higher than the senses, and beyond those elements is the mind, beyond the mind is the intellect, but above all is the *jiva* soul who transcends all others."

Thus, the highest aspect of any of us is the soul within. In fact, it is only due to the soul within that gives the body any value, any motivation or any life at all. Whatever we love or appreciate about anyone, it is only due to the soul within, and is actually the soul within which attracts us. This is further explained like this: "As the spokes of a wheel hold to the nave or hub, so does all this [all that we see around us] hold to spirit. That life moves by the spirit, and gives life to all. Father means spirit, mother means spirit, brother is spirit, sister is spirit, tutor is spirit, even the [great] Brahman is spirit." (*Chandogya Upanishad* 7.15.1)

In this wayThus, nothing we appreciate is without being touched by spirit, no matter whether it be someone we love, or someone we appreciate for their beauty, intelligence, strength, etc. It is only because they are touched by and connected with spirit that they have any beauty, ability, or life at all. Actually, it is the spirit that is the most worthy of all our appreciation in anyone. It is the subtle essence within us all. Just as the *Chandogya Upanishad* 4.12.1 & 4.13.1) explains, that though you cannot see the soul in the seed of the large trees, when it is planted properly it will be the cause of the growth of the tree. Similarly, just as when you take salt crystals and let them soak in a cup of water, they will disappear, you no longer see them. But when you taste the water, the presence of the salt becomes obvious. Similarly, you cannot directly see the soul with your eyes, but that subtle essence is obvious by witnessing the consciousness that pervades the body. How do you detect that consciousness? Because if you pinch any part of the body, it will produce pain, and due to the sense of self-preservation, the person or animal will move the body to prevent the pain. Thus, in any species of life, that sense of self-preservation is the evidence of the soul in that body. The soul is the real identity of the living entity.

As the *Bhagavad-gita* (13.34) describes, "As the sun alone illuminates this universe, similarly the soul, one within the body, illuminates the entire body by consciousness." Thus, it is the consciousness that pervades the body that is the evidence of the soul within.

In fact, the body is but the field of activities while in this material realm: "The five great elements [earth, air, fire, water, and ether], the false ego, intelligence, the unmanifested, the ten senses, the mind, the five sense objects, desire, hatred, happiness, distress, the aggregate, the life symptoms, and convictions–all these are considered, in summary, to be the field of activities and its interactions." (*Bg.* 13.6-7) These verses describe the exchanges that the soul experiences with and within the various elements and reactions in the material sphere of activity. Yes, as described in the previous chapter, the soul is beyond all these, especially when it regains its freedom in its natural spiritual position. Until then, due to misidentification with the material elements, it continues to undergo these constant changes due to its connection and identification with the body. But there is a way to become free, which we will describe later.

When we see ourselves as spirit soul within the body, then we can become free from all kinds of false designations. We are free from thinking we are a white or black body, or American or Russian, fat or skinny, intelligent or dumb, young or old, or even male or female. Yes, the soul is beyond being male or female according to the sex of the body. This may be a difficult concept for those who are not spiritually developed, but it becomes commonplace for anyone who begins to perceive the reality of who we really are. We may be dressed in so many ways, so many different types of clothes, but more importantly so many different types of bodies. But inside we are all the same. The soul, similar to all souls, looks different only according to the outer form or vehicle in which it exists. As spiritual beings, we are beyond all of these limitations or designations. The body is only the vehicle, a container, a space suit for living on this planet, but it is not who we really are. It is temporary and is not, and can never be, a permanent position. It is always changing. That is why a young skinny girl may later become an old fat granny. Or why a young intelligent executive may later become a reclusive cranky old man. It is the lesson therein that is trying to teach us not to get overly attached to a temporary identity that is not real. That which is temporary is never real. It is only an ever-changing state in which we find ourselves. The soul is eternal, as previously described, and that is what we are meant to find and understand. Otherwise, what have we really accomplished in this human existence?

* * *

Therefore, in summary, we need to understand that we are transcendental although in material bodies. It is necessary to recognize the difference between the body and soul. By first acquiring the knowledge and intelligence to discriminate the difference between the soul and the body, and then later by spiritual practice being able to actually see our spiritual identity, we can become free from the illusion of thinking we are these material bodies. Then we can actually see ourselves as limitless spiritual beings and attain the goal of this human existence, which is to reach the ultimate freedom of realizing our true spiritual identity. This is confirmed in the *Bhagavad-gita* (13.35): "One who knowingly sees this difference between the body and the owner of the body [the soul] and can understand the process of liberation from this bondage, also attains the supreme goal."

We must understand, as further related in the *Chandogya Upanishad* (8.1.5-6) that though the body may age, the spirit within does not. During the death of the body, the spirit soul does not die. That is the true identity of the living being. It is the self, free from sin, free from old age, free from death and grief, from hunger and thirst, which desires nothing but what it ought to desire, and imagines nothing but what it ought to imagine. However, while here on earth people follow as they are commanded [according to the dictates of their mind and senses], and depend on the object which they are attached to, be it a country, house or home, or a piece of land. And while in this existence on earth, whatever has been acquired by exertion [motivated work], perishes, along with whatever one has acquired for the next life through rituals or other pious actions that were performed. Those who depart from this world without having discovered the self, the soul, and those true desires, for them there is no freedom in all the worlds [for he remains attached to his bodily concept of life and all the desires and demands that go with it]. But those who depart from here after having discovered the self and those true [spiritual] desires, for them there is freedom in all the worlds. This means that one having realized his or her spiritual nature, there is nothing else to acquire, and such a person finds and exists in full freedom wherever they may go.

In this way, it can also be said that for such a person who has searched out and understood their true spiritual identity, he also obtains all the worlds and all desires. (*Chandogya Upanishad* 8.7.1) Thus, there is nothing left that this world can give them. They have already attained full freedom from such needs, such desires, and, thus, they already have everything that could be acquired anywhere. In other words, they have attained the ultimate fulfillment within themselves. In such a state, they have true contentment, which means happiness with them wherever they go. By focusing on their spiritual identity and their connection with the Supreme, they remain in full bliss at any given time.

CHAPTER SEVEN

The Supersoul

From the ancient Vedic texts, from the great sages, and even from our own deep meditation, we can learn that there is another presence within the body besides the soul, and that is the Supersoul, the expansion of the Supreme Being who is our ever-well-wishing friend who accompanies us wherever we go. He plays an extremely important part, of which the Vedic literature provides many descriptions. Of course, I am not relating all the verses that describe such details. I'm only giving the essential verses and views by which you can understand this information without being overwhelmed by all the references that can be found.

Practically speaking, the different systems of yoga are meant to unite the soul with the Supersoul. The word *yoga* is based on its root word, which is *yuj*, which means to connect with, to bind to or unite. And what is to be united? The soul with the Supersoul. And such forms of yoga as the Astanga yoga system, or Raja yoga, and other forms of yoga are meant to, ultimately, unite the soul and Supersoul. This is a basic principle. So, how do we begin to understand the Supersoul?

The first point is that beyond the soul within the body, as we have been discussing so far, is the Supersoul who is also within the body. As it is described, "The Supersoul [expansion of the Supreme] enters into the bodies of the created beings who are influenced by the modes of material nature and causes them to enjoy the effects of these modes by the subtle mind." (*Srimad-Bhagavatam* 1.2.33) In this way, it is this Supersoul who helps the individual beings find their way through this material labyrinth. The *jivas* are basically helpless in trying to attain their desires, and only with the help of the Supersoul can they begin to find some sort of material happiness, if that is what they want, even though it is so illusive.

The second point to understand is that, like the *jivatma* or individual spirit soul, the Supersoul exists in the heart. As the *Katha Upanishad* (2.6.17) relates, the Superself, not larger than a thumb, is always settled in the heart. Let us know Him, distinct from the *jivatma*, and draw forth that Self with steadiness, as one draws the pith from a reed. One should know Him as bright, immortal and blissful.

Or as Yamaraja continues to explain in the *Katha Upanishad* (1.2.20), the Supreme Atman is subtler than the subtle *jivatma*, it is almost impossible to trace Him out. He is still greater than the greatest, and is immanent in the core of the hearts of all beings. One who is free from all desires of salvation and elevation [within this universe], but practices unalloyed devotion [bhakti yoga], then and then alone by the grace of the Supreme unto him can that person realize that Supreme Divinity, and then rise above all sorrows.

The *Mundaka Upanishad* (2.2.1) confirms it in this way, saying that the Supreme Being is self-effulgent and remains ever dwelling in the core of the heart, for which He is known as Guhachara [moving in the cavity of one's being]. He is the final resort for all beings that move, breathe or wink. Know Him as the very cause of both the gross and the subtle, the transcendent and mundane. He is the Supreme adorable, the highest object and inconceivable by human intellect.

The *Chandogya Upanishad* (8.3.3) and the *Brihadaranyaka Upanishad* (4.4.22) also verifies that the Superself is He who resides in the heart, the unborn Self who consists of knowledge, within the heart surrounded by the *pranas* or life airs.

Next, we can understand the size, shape, and dress of the Supersoul, who is realized and seen by those sages who

The Supersoul

have reached the goal of knowledge through yoga. This is also described in *Srimad-Bhagavatam* as follows: "Others conceive of the Personality of Godhead residing within the body in the region of the heart and measuring only eight inches, with four hands carrying a lotus, a *chakra*, a conch shell and a club respectively. His mouth expresses His happiness. His eyes spread like the petals of a lotus, and His garments, yellowish like the saffron of the *kadamba* flower, are bedecked with valuable jewels. His ornaments are all made of gold, set with jewels, and He wears a glowing head-dress and earrings. His lotus feet are placed over the whorls of the lotus-like hearts of great mystics. On His chest is the Kaustubha jewel, engraved with a beautiful calf, and there are other jewels on His shoulders. His complete torso is garlanded with fresh flowers. He is well decorated with an ornamental wreath about His waist and rings studded with valuable jewels on His fingers. His leglets, His bangles, His oiled hair, curling with a bluish tint, and His beautiful smiling face are all very pleasing. The Lord's magnanimous pastimes and the glowing glancing of His smiling face are all indications of His extensive benedictions. One must therefore concentrate on this transcendental form of the Lord, as long as the mind can be fixed on Him by meditation." (*Bhag*.2.2.8-12)

How to perceive the presence of the Supersoul within the body is through one of three ways: by perfection in meditation, by cultivation of knowledge, or by engaging in the process of yoga. Others can understand the Supersoul by hearing this knowledge from spiritual authorities. In any case, if one attains such spiritual vision he will actually see things as they are and the transcendental destination then becomes achievable.

Further ways of recognizing the Supersoul has to do with how He integrates the body and soul. This is described in the *Taittiriya Upanishad* (3.10.2). It is pointed out that one can perceive the Supersoul by the action of speech, as action in the hands, and walking in the feet and other bodily activities. This is further substantiated in *Srimad-Bhagavatam* (2.2.35) where it states: "The Personality of Godhead Lord Sri Krishna is in every living being [as Supersoul] along with the individual soul. And this fact is perceived and hypothesized in our acts of seeing and taking help from intelligence." Therefore, through the Vedic literature we can understand that the unifying factor between the desires of the self or soul and the response of the brain and body to our desires can be recognized as the power of the Supersoul within. It is the Supersoul who creates the unifying effect between the individual soul and the actions of the body.

To begin establishing what is the integrating mechanism between the soul and the body, the Vedic literature explains that in addition to the conscious self that is existing within the body, there is also a higher principle of consciousness--Superconsciousness or Supersoul. So, on one side you have the gross material body, including the brain and senses, along with the subtle body of mind, intelligence and false ego. On the other side you have the conscious self or spirit soul. Then what integrates the self and makes it so attuned to the gross and subtle body is that which is between them, known as the Supersoul.

So, this Superconsciousness or Supersoul is able to unify the machinery of the body and the conscious self. Without the presence of the Supersoul, it is not possible. In other words, the conscious self is dependent on the Superself for it to have the power to use its body, brain and intelligence in the way that it wants. Otherwise, the soul is simply existing within the body without any means of interacting or expressing itself through the vehicle of the body. In this way, the Supersoul gives us the power to move our body or have a collective consciousness that extends throughout the body to where we think "I am," "I am this body," or "This body is me." Then, under the influence of the bodily ego, this expands into thinking that I am a white body, a black body, and I come from this country, I belong to a certain culture, and I am dedicated to this way of thinking and so on. Thus, the false ego, or the ego based on the bodily identification, expands to no end in how it begins to think of itself and accept things as a part of him, though they are all of a temporary nature. But still, such a conditioned soul takes it all so seriously.

The Supersoul also guides the individual souls, although He does not personally take part in fulfilling their desires. He arranges the fulfillment of such desires by the workings of material nature. The living entities are independent in the respect that they are free to desire whatever they want, no matter whether they be uplifting or degrading. Only the Supreme allows them to fulfill their desires, but the Supreme is never responsible for the actions and reactions of the situations which may be desired by the living entities. In other words, as the living beings pursue their various desires by the power the Supersoul has given them, they must realize that this universe is governed by certain laws which the Supreme has established and set in motion. If we perform activities that break those laws, particular reactions will automatically follow. The Lord is neutral to everyone and does not interfere with the desires of the living beings. We, therefore, cannot blame God for those reactions that we will have to endure which were caused by our own unlawful desires. And, as they say, ignorance of the law is no excuse.

Because of their various good or bad activities, the living entities get what they deserve and are carried by the material energy to either happiness or misery, as experienced by the body. A person may not remember all of his or her good or evil deeds, but the Supersoul can remember everything we have done either in this life or any other previous life. The Supreme, through previously established universal laws, thus causes material nature automatically to award or punish the living beings accordingly, though He remains above it all. He only supplies the knowledge by which, if used properly, the living beings can decide what is best for them to do. Once they decide what they want, then it is the Supersoul which gives them the facility. Therefore, one Vedic hymn states: "The Lord engages the living entity in pious activities so he may be elevated. The Lord engages one in impious activities so he may go to hell. The living entity is completely dependent in one's distress and happiness. By the will of the Supreme one can go to heaven or hell as a cloud is driven by the air." A similar statement is also found in the *Kaushitaki Upanishad* (3.8).

This, of course, does not mean that God decides where one will go, but it is based on the desires of the living entity. To fulfill the desires of the living being, the Lord guides him or her in a certain way. Thus, the Supreme guides and empowers the living beings to act according to their desires and then witnesses all the activities that they perform. In this way, the living beings can act out their wishes, but must still face the reactions of their activities.

Through all this enjoyment or suffering, the Supersoul is the individual soul's constant companion. As previously stated, if the living beings, after becoming exhausted from the continuous ups and downs of happiness and distress, look toward their friend the Supersoul, they can be relieved from all suffering which has been caused by their misguided actions. At that time, the Supersoul helps the conditioned soul by giving real intelligence for understanding one's ever-blissful, spiritual position. However, the ability for one to perceive the Supersoul depends on one's sincerity to advance spiritually:

"O King Yudhisthira, the Supersoul in every body gives intelligence to the individual soul according to his capacity for understanding. Therefore, the Supersoul is the chief within the body. The Supersoul is manifested to the individual soul according to the individual's comparative development of knowledge, austerity, penance, and so on." (*Bhag.*7.14.38)

Therefore, we get further explanations as to the location and even some of the character and purpose of the Supersoul that exists within us all. But how do we relieve ourselves from the constant ups and downs of life that we undergo because of our misguided aim of life? How does the Supersoul help us?

In the *Svetashvatarara Upanishad* (4.6-7), *Mundaka Upanishad* (3.1.1-3) as well as the *Srimad-Bhagavatam* (11.11.6-7) we find that the body is like a tree, and within this tree there are two birds who exist as inseparable friends clinging in the branches. One of the birds eats of the fruits of the tree [the good or bad, sweet or sour results of the actions that are performed with the body]. The other bird [the Supersoul] perfectly understands His own position and that of the conditioned living being. He is eternally liberated and simply looks on like a witness. The eating bird, who does not understand his spiritual position or the Lord, sits there immersed in grief, bewildered by his actions and the results thereof. But when he gazes toward the other bird, the Lord or Supersoul, who is content and merely looking on, then his grief passes away. Then he can shake off good and evil, cut asunder the knot of worldly bondage, and dwell in the Self, and he reaches the highest oneness with God, free from passions.

Therefore, once we begin to understand how illusive material happiness can be, or how we are often left still feeling unsatisfied regardless of how much we have attempted to fulfill our desires, by looking toward our eternal friend the Supersoul, we can again begin to move toward perceiving our true spiritual nature. When we are ready to get serious about regaining our actual spiritual identity, the Supersoul in the heart will begin to guide us toward making ever-increasing spiritual progress. Any inspiration that we get for this insight and perception comes from the Supersoul within. As it is explained in the *Srimad-Bhagavatam* (7.2.45), the most important thing in the body for our chance of living is the life airs [*pranas*] within us, but that also is neither the listener nor the speaker. In other words, it is inert. And beyond that the soul also can do nothing, for the Supersoul is actually the director of our activities and even our bodily functions, in cooperation with the [desires of the] individual soul. The Supersoul who conducts the activities of the body is different from both the body, the *pranas*, and the living force or soul.

Once having understood the Supersoul in the heart, or even knowing that he is existing there, a person should never forget his or her situation or the causeless compassion of the Supersoul for always being our companion in all the activities that we undergo, whether for good or evil. Or, as it is explained in the *Srimad-Bhagavatam* (11.8.31): "I am such a fool that I have given up the service of that person who, being eternally situated within my heart, is actually most dear to me. That most dear one is the Lord of the universe, who is the bestower of real love and happiness, and the source of all prosperity. Although He is in my own heart, I have completely neglected Him. Instead I have ignorantly served insignificant men who can never satisfy my real desires and who have simply brought me unhappiness, fear, anxiety, lamentation, and illusion."

CHAPTER EIGHT

Spiritual Perception

When it comes to actually perceiving the soul, it is clearly understood that you cannot do that with the material senses. The *Brihadaranyaka Upanishad* (2.3.4) relates that the eye sees what is material. Thus, you have to go beyond the means of the senses to see what is spiritual. You have to see the self through knowledge, meditation, or through experience in perceiving that which is in the spiritual strata. In one of these ways you may see the spiritual spark within all beings.

However, until we are able to directly see the soul within, the *Upanishads* also describe other ways in which we can see the influence of the soul. We can also see the self within the body due to the fact that the body is functioning. Without a soul, the body has no life. Thus, when we perceive the actions of the body, such as speech, sight, hearing, thinking, hunger, thirst, movement, the pumping of the heart, the breathing, etc., all of these are bodily activities by which we are witnessing evidence of the soul within the body.

Also, anyone that we hold dear, and anything that we appreciate about them, such as their beauty, strength, knowledge, intelligence, mannerisms, are but different forms of evidence of the soul within. Thus, anything that we admire in anyone is because of the soul within. This may include a husband, a wife, children, or others such as entertainers that we like and appreciate. Thus, what is of utmost value is not the body, but the soul within.

In this way, we can understand that, ultimately, it is

really only the soul that we hold dear, for without that, the body dies and deteriorates. But such feelings of appreciation or love are but emotions to be expressed, filtered through our mind and body toward the object of our admiration or affection. And if we cannot express such emotions, then they become bottled up and we long for showing such expressions, even if we have to get a pet to have around the house so we can exhibit such feelings towards it. Thus, such feelings, though expressions of the mind, are again but reflections of the loving nature of the soul within. This is the character of the soul, and is how we can perceive the soul in everyone and in all kinds of living beings. Only due to the self within is there any reason for someone to be dear to us. This is but one of the ways we can recognize the soul within.

As the *Isha Upanishad* (Mantra 7) explains, "One who always sees all living entities as spiritual sparks, in quality one with the Lord, becomes a true knower of things. What, then, can be illusion for him?" This vision, of seeing all living beings as spiritual in essence, is the means of becoming truly free from the illusion, and also being a seer of the spiritual reality.

The *Bhagavad-gita* (6.32) further describes, "He is a perfect yogi who, by compassion to his own self, sees the true equality of all beings, both in their happiness and distress." The thing is that the only way to recognize the true equality amongst us all is to see our spiritual identity. Materially, anyone can see there are so many differences between us, and focusing on those means that we will never see the equality between us. But here it is explained that the only way to really see our unity is by recognizing our spiritual identity, which is the same in all of us. Once we can do that, we can see beyond our physical characteristics, our material differences, beyond our mindsets, our religions, our race, age, sex, etc. Only then can we begin to understand who and what we really are and how we all must work together because, essentially speaking, we are all the same.

However, even beyond this, it is described that "He who sees everything in relation to the Supreme Lord, who sees all entities as His parts and parcels, and who sees the Supreme Lord within everything, never hates anything nor any being." (*Isha Upanishad*, Mantra 6) Over and above seeing the spiritual nature of all beings, seeing how the Supreme is in everything and in every being puts one in touch with the Supreme Reality at all times, regardless of your situation. Then, naturally, how can you hate anyone or anything when you can see it is connected with God? Or, as it is questioned, what is not God? This means that we need to see how everything is but a display of the energy of God. Then, when you have this perception, all aspects of life become a positive part of bringing you into higher levels of thought and consciousness. It is only that which continues to promote or perpetuate the illusion that leads you to improper vision, inappropriate actions, and is the cause of suffering. But this is easily corrected when you have spiritual perception. When you know who and what you really are, then you truly know what to do with yourself. When you can see the reality of all beings, the reality of life, then you know its real purpose. Otherwise you remain in a confused condition, as described:

"Sometimes you think yourself a man, sometimes a chaste woman, or sometimes a neutral eunuch. This is all because of the body, which is created by the illusory energy. This illusory energy is My potency, and actually both of us–you and I–are pure spiritual identities. Now just try to understand this. I am trying to explain our factual position." (*Bhag*.4.28.61) Here the Supreme is describing the spiritual similarities between us and Him, but because we wrongly identify ourselves as the body, we have strong misconceptions of who we are. This is what must be adjusted before we can have spiritual perception.

The first step in changing our perception is to realize the soul is beyond all material conceptions and representations. And one who has realized the soul knows this. "When the luminaries in the sky, such as the moon, the sun and the stars, are reflected in liquids like oil or water, they appear to be of different shapes–sometimes round, sometimes long, [or shaky], and so on–because of the movements of the wind [which effect the water]. Similarly, when the living entity, the soul, is absorbed in materialistic thoughts, he accepts various manifestations as his own identity because of ignorance. In other words, one is bewildered by mental concoctions because of agitation from the material modes of nature." (*Bhag*.10.1.43)

In this way, our view of things changes because of the temporary and ever-transforming nature of the material energy. Yet, when the living being returns to or regains his or her spiritual consciousness, he rises above his material conceptions, which are the cause of his continued existence in the illusion. Then he becomes blissful in spiritual perception, which is his real constitutional position. "One who is thus transcendentally situated at once realizes the Supreme Brahman and becomes fully joyful. He never laments nor desires to have anything; he is equally disposed to every living entity. In that state, he attains pure devotional service to Me [the Supreme]." (*Bg*.18.54) In this way, the living being regains his natural spiritual occupation. He knows his real identity, his actual position, and his normal state of consciousness, and his vocation as a spirit soul. Then there is no more confusion, but only great bliss as a spiritual being in contact with the Supreme Spirit. Nothing can be of greater joy than this. This is the ultimate freedom. And this is summarized as follows:

"One who is enlightened in self-realization, although living within the material body, sees himself as transcendental to the body, just as one who has arisen from a dream gives up identification with the dream body. A foolish person, however, although not identical with his material body but transcendental to it, thinks himself to be the physical form,

Spiritual Perception

just as one who is dreaming sees himself as situated in an imaginary body." (*Bhag*.11.11.8)

In this way, one who is beginning to attain spiritual perception knows that he is different from the body. He can sense it, feel it, and, with practice on the spiritual path, finally see it. Just as one who observes the birth of a tree from its seed and its ultimate death is separate from the tree itself, in the same way, one who witnesses the birth and death of the material body, even his own, remains separate from it. (*Bhag*.11.22.50)

In this way, the person or soul is the witness of life, watching the body go through the constant changes that are inevitable on the material platform. As in a dream, all material feelings have no essential reality in material existence because they are not necessarily connected with the soul. It is only that which is directly connected with the soul that has any reality or lasts forever. Everything that is material rises and falls, or comes and goes. Thus, one must know that he is always different from the actions and reactions of the material body and mind, or even mental expressions, which are but projections of the desire to satisfy the senses. They are but like swirls of smoke in the air that ever-change and gradually fade into something else. As a spiritual being, however, the soul is above all of this. When a person begins to actually perceive this, he no longer has such a keen interest to engage the body in expressing such materially based emotions, or in merely gratifying the senses to experience sensual thrills, all of which are like temporary swirls of smoke, always changing and fading away. He knows that the identity of the soul is nothing material. "The material body made of earth is not the true self; nor are the senses, their presiding demigods, or the air of life [within the body]; nor is the external air, water or fire, or one's mind. All these are simply matter. Similarly, neither one's intelligence, material consciousness nor ego, nor the elements of ether or earth, nor the objects of sense perception, nor even the primeval state of material equilibrium to be considered the actual identity of the soul." (*Bhag*.11.28.24)

The material elements and all that is temporary is simply part of nature. Nature means neutral, it simply does what it is supposed to do. It will neither drag one down, or lift one up. It is only our consciousness that does that. We determine our own progress or lack thereof by our own state of mind. If we see the Supreme in all aspects of nature, that it is part of His energy, such an understanding and vision can lift us up, always. But, nonetheless, as spiritual beings who desire complete freedom from material limitations, identifying ourselves with the material energy will keep us from experiencing the unlimited spiritual bliss that we long for. That can only be experienced by understanding and perceiving ourselves as spirit souls, part of the eternal spiritual energy, who are above and beyond anything that is material, anything that has a birth and death, a beginning or end. As the *Katha Upanishad* (2.5.11-12) relates, "As the sun, the eye of the whole world, is not contaminated by the external impurities seen by the eyes, similarly the one self within all things is never contaminated by the misery of the world, being above them. There is one ruler, the self within all things... The wise who perceive him within, to them belongs eternal happiness, not to others."

This is the key to the eternal bliss that is discussed in the Vedic texts. One who is naturally aware and perceives his own spiritual identity, and the same in all other beings, and also recognizes the Divine in all beings as the Supersoul, is practically already liberated from material existence. He will not need to return to take birth in another material body. He has attained the goal of life in this universe. "Such a liberated person is not attracted to material sense pleasure or external objects but is always in trance, enjoying the pleasure within. In this way, the self-realized person enjoys unlimited happiness, for he concentrates on the Supreme." (*Bg*.5.21)

On this same thought, the *Taittiriya Upanishad* (2.9.1)

goes on to describe that one who knows the bliss of Brahman [the spiritual nature within and around us], fears nothing. He frees himself through such knowledge and spiritual perception.

* * *

In conclusion, we should understand that as we progress on our spiritual path, performing our *sadhana* or spiritual practices for uplifting and spiritualizing our consciousness, and gradually discerning the difference between the illusion and spiritual reality, and becoming more aware of our spiritual nature and identity, we should continue to work in this way as we go through life in order to attain complete entrance into the spiritual domain. This is also described in the *Srimad-Bhagavatam* (11.13.35): "Having understood the temporary nature of material things, and thus having pulled one's vision away from illusion, one should remain without material desires. By experiencing the happiness of the soul, one should give up material speaking and activities. If sometimes one must observe the material world, one should remember that it is not the ultimate reality and, therefore, one has given it up. By such constant remembrance up till the time of death, one will not again fall into illusion."

This is how one attains complete liberation from material existence, to the extent of never having to take birth in the material worlds again. After all, most of what we do here in this world is simply for maintaining this body. It must be fed, it has to drink, it must be clothed and sheltered, and for that we have to have a job to work for money to maintain our economic development, defend our position and belongings and whatever wealth we may have accumulated, and find some place for shelter. Such a life is actually great trouble and anxiety. So, if we can be free of this, then who would not want to leave it behind for something better? But we simply have to know how to reach that something better. We have to be shown the way. And once we have been given the instructions on how to do that, then we need to take it very seriously. Such an opportunity for this kind of spiritual knowledge may only come once in a lifetime, or not even after many lifetimes. Therefore, we should come to understand clearly that this world does not have the value that many people place on it. It is a place where we should learn what is necessary, acquire the spiritual knowledge we need, and then act on it to make sure we do not have to stay any longer than necessary in this realm. That is the result of attaining genuine spiritual perception, and the real goal of human life.

CHAPTER NINE

Life After Death

Death is the final test when we see exactly what the cumulative affect of our consciousness is and where it will take us. Many people are afraid of death, and rightly so. They do not know what they will find or where they will go. So, it is of concern to them, and to anyone else who has the intelligence to know the importance of such a transition. It is our consciousness and the actions of our life, or karma, which will determine where we go after death. Thus, the next life we enter is given according to what we want, what we desire, combined with what we deserve.

Some people say they are not afraid of death or have no regard for it, but they are fools unless they have already seen the other side of life and know what they will experience there. They will still be taken somewhere, and that most people do not know because they either have not prepared for it, or do not want to think about it. But it is like the mundane laws of the courts. People may follow them or not, and may even get away with breaking the laws for many years. But once they get caught, it no longer matters if they believe in the laws or not, they must still face the consequences for their actions. Then they will be thrown into the jail for their crimes whether they like it or not.

It has been said that death is that journey from which no one returns. But, by developing oneself spiritually, a person can determine which way he will go after death, upward or downward, and, thus, help prepare himself or herself to reach the best situation in the next life. This is a major point regarding the purpose of our spiritual development so that we can maintain as much focus as possible during the mental and physical turbulence that often accompanies the experience of death, depending on how we leave the body. We may drift out of the body in a natural sort of way, or go through situations that force us out. This will make a difference in how well we can handle the transition. But we must also be aware of the fact that we could die at any time. Life is fragile, and preparation is the key for any man of wisdom.

The *Brihadaranyaka Upanishad* (4.4.2-4) gives a brief summary of what happens at death. It explains that the point of the heart where the veins and subtle channels called the *nadis* go out of the heart becomes lighted up, like a tunnel lit at the end, and by that light the self departs through certain points, such as the top of the skull, the eye, or through other openings of the body. When he departs, the life airs or *pranas* go with him. The soul follows at which time both his knowledge or consciousness and his karma, or the result of his actions, and his familiarity with former things also take hold of him.

Afterwards, as a caterpillar reaches the end of blade of grass and reaches out for another, so does the soul, after having thrown off his present body, begin to draw himself toward another life. Or, as a goldsmith takes a piece of gold and turns it into another newer and more beautiful shape, so does the self, after having thrown off the present body, makes himself another newer and more beautiful form, whether it be like the ancestors, or the Gandharvas [angels], or like the *devas* [demigods], or like Brahma, or other beings. In this way, a person develops as he behaves in this life. A man of good acts will become good, and a man of bad acts will go downward into lower births, lower species of life. He becomes pure by pure deeds, and bad by bad deeds. Thus, it is the progressive development of one's consciousness which brings one to increasingly higher forms of life, while lower thoughts and actions will take one to increasingly lower forms or species of life. So, after death a person may acquire a human form, or live in the subtle realm for some time before taking another human birth, or occupy a different species of life altogether. Even the subtle realm has different levels, some higher or heavenly and others lower or even hellish. We acquire the kind of situation that best suites our consciousness.

The *Katha Upanishad* (2.6.16) also adds, "There are one hundred and one arteries of the heart, one of them penetrates the crown of the head. Moving upwards through it, a man (at his death) reaches the Immortal. The other arteries serve to take one in different directions." This reveals that the way one leaves the body will determine the level of good or bad the next life will be. If one goes through the upward arteries, such as through the skull, it is likely that the next life will be higher and auspicious. But if one is lead through a downward pointing artery, such as forcing the soul and life airs to leave through such openings as the anus or some other orifice, then the next life is likely to be less advantageous or even inauspicious.

The *Katha Upanishad* (2.5.7) also states that a person may, after death, enter a womb in order to acquire another organic body, while others may go into inorganic matter according to their work and according to their consciousness. So, if a person is too wicked, he may acquire a body that will be extremely constrictive in order to reduce the activity and harm that such person will ever be able to do again.

Therefore, it is "By means of thoughts, touching, seeing, and passions that the incarnate self assumes successively in various places and various forms, in accordance with his actions, just as the body grows when food and drink are given to it. That incarnate self, according to his own qualities, chooses many shapes, whether gross or subtle. Having himself caused his appearance in them, he is seen consecutively in one form after another, through the qualities of his actions [and consciousness]." (*Svetashvatara Upanishad* 5.12)

According to this, we choose, according to our consciousness, which is formed by our thoughts, words and deeds in this life, the kinds of life forms in which we will appear. And we appear in these forms in the consecutive order which accommodates our karma and the need to work out our desires and just deserts. These forms may be in the gross, physical world or in the subtle realm. Thus, one lifetime may indeed create the karma that requires a consecutive order of lives in the future to allow it to be worked out. It is as if we are writing our own book to be lived in the future. No one else is to blame. Thus, we must be serious about making sure we do not trap ourselves in such a way, but work to attain spiritual advancement that can keep us free from such a fate.

Otherwise, as it is further explained, "There are indeed those unblessed worlds, covered with blind darkness. Men who are ignorant and not enlightened [with spiritual knowledge] go after death to those worlds." (*Brihadaranyaka Upanishad* 4.4.11) Thus, we find the importance in this verse for the reason to make spiritual progress in our lives. But more importantly is to reach reality, the spiritual dimension based on who and what we really are, for that is all that can completely satisfy the soul, our real identity. That is our real home for which everyone is looking, whether they realize it or not.

* * *

In conclusion, the point to understand is that it is only spiritual knowledge and self-realization that can deliver a person from continued births in the material realm. Faith alone in something is a start, but it is not enough. As the *Katha Upanishad* (2.6.4) specifically points out, "If a man could not understand it before the falling asunder of his body, then he has to take another body in the worlds of creation." This shows how important it is to take this opportunity of human life seriously for developing deep spiritual understanding.

Thus, "At the last stage of one's life, one should be bold enough not to be afraid of death. But one must cut off all attachments to the material body and everything pertaining to it, and all desires thereof." (*Bhag.*2.1.15) In this way, it is the desire for bodily pleasures that keep one attached to the body, and causes one to continue in the rounds of birth and death on the material platform of life. Being free from such desires opens the door to eternal freedom. And there is no more powerful of a way to do this than to take shelter of deep spiritual knowledge and the process of spiritual realization.

After all, "If a man understands the self, saying 'I am he,' what could he wish or desire for by hankering after the body?" (*Brihadaranyaka Upanishad* 4.4.12)

Therefore, the higher our state of consciousness, the higher our next life will be, which is also explained as follows: "Whatever state of being one remembers when he quits his body, that state he will attain without fail." (*Bg.*8.6) Thus, the next form after death that we attain is given to us to properly fit our state of mind or consciousness that we had attained by the time of our death. This way, in our next life, we continue in the direction we established in this life, ether higher or lower, or the same. Or, as explained further by Lord Krishna, "By becoming fixed in this knowledge, one can attain to the transcendental nature, which is like My own nature. Thus established, one is not born [again] at the time of creation, nor disturbed at the time of dissolution." (*Bg.*14.2)

The most important thing is that, as spiritual beings, the more we think of or meditate on the Supreme Spirit, the more spiritual our consciousness will be, and the more likely we will reach the supreme destination, the perfection of human life. This is not impossible, but only requires sincerity, and steady determination. As stated in the *Bhagavad-gita*

(8.5), "And whoever, at the time of death, quits his body remembering Me alone, at once attains My nature. Of this there is no doubt." Thus, the person with a fully spiritual consciousness will certainly reach the spiritual domain. Nothing can be better than this for any spiritual aspirant.

Conclusion

Herein is the summery of some of the deepest spiritual understanding known to mankind. It is the key knowledge for spiritual awakening. There is much more information that is available on this topic, and it expands into many branches to cover all aspects of life and every way of looking at spiritual truth. If you go through the Vedic library of texts that have been provided, you will find that there are also many levels of spiritual understanding that are discussed, and various methods of spiritual practice for self-realization.

I have not delved deeply into that aspect of the spiritual discussion in this book in order to keep it simple. But I have provided the next level of understanding in other books I have written, as described on the pages that follow. These are especially meant to help make what some may consider complex topics into easy to understand explanations and procedures to follow.

Also, one should be sure to read some of the Vedic texts, such as *Bhagavad-gita*, *Isha Upanishad*, or even the *Bhagavata Purana* (*Srimad-Bhagavatam*), though that can be a little lengthy for some. You should also look into how to practice yoga, especially bhakti yoga, the art of union with the Supreme through love and devotion, and mantra yoga, or the chanting of the holy names of God, etc., which are considered some of the easiest but most important processes of self-realization for this age.

I especially wish the readers of this book the best for their spiritual development. The information presented here is a summary of some of the most important information I studied when I first started delving more deeply into this spiritual knowledge. It changed my life forever, and once started, I just had to keep going further and further into it. And I am sure it can do the same for you.

GLOSSARY

Acharya--the spiritual master who sets the proper standard by his own example.

Advaita--nondual, meaning that the Absolute is one with the infinitesimal souls with no individuality between them. The philosophy of Sankaracharya.

Agni--fire, or Agni the demigod of fire.

Ahankara--false ego, identification with matter.

Ananda--spiritual bliss.

Ananta--unlimited.

Arati--the ceremony of worship when incense and ghee lamps are offered to the Deities.

Arca-vigraha--the worshipable Deity form of the Lord made of stone, wood, etc. Aryan--a noble person, one who is on the path of spiritual advancement.

Asana--postures for meditation, or exercises for developing the body into a fit instrument for spiritual advancement.

Asat--that which is temporary.

Ashrama--one of the four orders of spiritual life, such as *brahmachari* (celibate student), *grihastha* (married householder), *vanaprastha* (retired stage), and *sannyasa* (renunciate); or the abode of a spiritual teacher or *sadhu*.

Asura--one who is ungodly or a demon.

Atma--the self or soul. Sometimes means the body, mind, and senses.

Atman--usually referred to as the Supreme Self.

Avatara--an incarnation of the Lord who descends from the spiritual world.

Avidya--ignorance or nescience.

Aum--om or *pranava*

Ayurveda--the original holistic form of medicine as described in the Vedic literature.

Bhajan--song of worship.

Bhakta--a devotee of the Lord who is engaged in *bhakti yoga*.

Bhakti--love and devotion for God.

Bhakti yoga--the path of offering pure devotional service to the

Glossary

Supreme.

Bhava--preliminary stage of love of God.

Brahma--the demigod of creation who was born from Lord Vishnu, the first created living being and the engineer of the secondary stage of creation of the universe when all the living entities were manifested.

Brahmachari--a celebate student who is trained by the spiritual master. One of the four divisions or ashramas of spiritual life.

Brahmajyoti--the great white light or effulgence which emanates from the body of the Lord.

Brahmaloka--the highest planet or plane of existence in the universe; the planet where Lord Brahma lives.

Brahman--the spiritual energy; the all-pervading impersonal aspect of the Lord; or the Supreme Lord Himself.

Brahmana or brahmin--one of the four orders of society; the intellectual class of men who have been trained in the knowledge of the *Vedas* and initiated by a spiritual master.

Brahmana--the supplemental books of the four primary *Vedas*. They usually contained instructions for performing Vedic *agnihotras*, chanting the *mantras*, the purpose of the rituals, etc. The *Aitareya* and *Kaushitaki Brahmanas* belong to the *Rig-veda*, the *Satapatha Brahmana* belongs to the *White Yajur-veda*, and the *Taittiriya Brahmana* belongs to the *Black Yajur-veda*. The *Praudha* and *Shadvinsa Brahmanas* are two of the eight *Brahmanas* belonging to the *Atharva-veda*.

Caitanya Mahaprabhu--the most recent incarnation of the Lord who appeared in the 15th century in Bengal and who originally started the *sankirtana* movement, based on congregational chanting of the holy names.

Causal Ocean or Karana Ocean--is the corner of the spiritual sky where Maha-Vishnu lies down to create the material manifestation.

Chakra--a wheel, disk, or psychic energy center situated along the spinal column in the subtle body of the physical shell.

Cit--eternal knowledge.

Darshan--the devotional act of seeing and being seen by the Deity in the temple.

Deity--the *arca-vigraha*, or worshipful form of the Supreme in the temple, or deity as the worshipful image of the demigod. A capital D is used in referring to Krishna or one of His expansions, while a small d is used when referring to a demigod or lesser personality.

Devas--demigods or heavenly beings from higher levels of material existence, or a godly person.

Devaloka--the higher planets or planes of existence of the devas.

Dham--a holy place.

Dharma--the essential nature or duty of the living being.

Dualism--as related in this book refers to the Supreme as both an impersonal force as well as a person.

Dvapara-yuga--the third age which lasts 864,000 years.

Dwaita--dualism, the principle that the Absolute Truth consists of the infinite Supreme Being and the infinitesimal individual souls.

Gandharvas--the celestial angel-like beings who have beautiful forms and voices, and are expert in dance and music, capable of becoming invisible and can help souls on the earthly plane.

Ganesh--a son of Shiva, said to destroy obstacles (as Vinayaka) and offer good luck to those who petition him.

Ganges--the sacred and spiritual river which, according to the *Vedas*, runs throughout the universe, a portion of which is seen in India. The reason the river is considered holy is that it is said to be a drop of the Karana Ocean that leaked in when Lord Vishnu, in His incarnation as Vamanadeva, kicked a small hole in the universal shell with His toe. Thus, the water is spiritual as well as being purified by the touch of Lord Vishnu.

Gangotri--the source of the Ganges River in the Himalayas.

Garbhodakasayi Vishnu--the expansion of Lord Vishnu who enters into each universe.

Gaudiya--a part of India sometimes called Aryavarta or land of the Aryans, located south of the Himalayas and north of the Vindhya Hills.

Gayatri--the spiritual vibration or *mantra* from which the other

Vedas were expanded and which is chanted by those
who are initiated as *brahmanas* and given the spiritual
understanding of Vedic philosophy.

Goloka Vrindavana--the name of Lord Krishna's spiritual planet.

Gosvami--one who is master of the senses.

Govinda--a name of Krishna which means one who gives
pleasure to the cows and senses.

Guru--a spiritual master.

Hare--the Lord's pleasure potency, Radharani, who is
approached for accessibility to the Lord.

Hari--a name of Krishna as the one who takes away one's
obstacles on the spiritual path.

Haribol--a word that means to chant the name of the Lord, Hari.

Harinam--refers to the name of the Lord, Hari.

Hiranyagarbha--another name of Brahma who was born of
Vishnu in the primordial waters within the egg of the
universe.

Hrishikesa--a name for Krishna which means the master of the
senses.

Impersonalism--the view that God has no personality or form,
but is only an impersonal force.

Impersonalist--those who believe God has no personality or
form.

Incarnation--the taking on of a body or form.

Indra--the King of heaven and controller of rain, who by his
great power conquers the forces of darkness.

Jiva--the individual soul or living being.

Jivanmukta--a liberated soul, though still in the material body
and universe.

Jiva-shakti--the living force.

Jnana-kanda--the portion of the *Vedas* which stresses empirical
speculation for understanding truth.

Jnana yoga--the process of linking with the Supreme through
empirical knowledge and mental speculation.

Kala--eternal time.

Kali--the demigoddess who is the fierce form of the wife of Lord
Shiva. The word *kali* comes from *kala*, the Sanskrit
word for time: the power that destroys everything.

Kali-yuga--the fourth and present age, the age of quarrel and confusion, which lasts 432,000 years and began 5,000 years ago.

Kalpa--a day in the life of Lord Brahma which lasts a thousand cycles of the four *yugas*.

Karanodakasayi Vishnu (Maha-Vishnu)--the expansion of Lord Krishna who created all the material universes.

Karma--material actions performed in regard to developing one's position or for future results which produce *karmic* reactions. It is also the reactions one endures from such fruitive activities.

Karma-kanda--the portion of the *Vedas* which primarily deals with recommended fruitive activities for various results.

Karma-yoga--the system of yoga for dovetailing one's activities for spiritual advancement.

Kirtana--chanting or singing the glories of the Lord.

Krishna--the name of the original Supreme Personality of Godhead which means the most attractive and greatest pleasure. He is the source of all other incarnations, such as Vishnu, Rama, Narasimha, Narayana, Buddha, Parashurama, Vamanadeva, Kalki at the end of Kali-yuga, etc.

Krishnaloka--the spiritual planet where Lord Krishna resides.

Kshatriya--the second class of *varna* of society, or occupation of administrative or protective service, such as warrior or military personnel.

Ksirodakasayi Vishnu--the Supersoul expansion of the Lord who enters into each atom and the heart of each individual.

Lakshmi--the goddess of fortune and wife of Lord Vishnu.

Lila--pastimes.

Lilavataras--the many incarnations of God who appear to display various spiritual pastimes to attract the conditioned souls in the material world.

Linga--the shapeless form of Lord Shiva.

Mahabharata--the great epic of the Pandavas, which includes the *Bhagavad-gita*, by Vyasadeva.

Maha-mantra--the best mantra for self-realization in this age, called the Hare Krishna mantra.

Mahat-tattva--the total material energy.

Maha-Vishnu or Karanodakasayi Vishnu--the Vishnu expansion

of Lord Krishna from whom all the material universes emanate.

Mandir--a temple.

Mantra--a sound vibration which prepares the mind for spiritual realization and delivers the mind from material inclinations. In some cases a mantra is chanted for specific material benefits.

Maya--illusion, or anything that appears to not be connected with the eternal Absolute Truth.

Mayavadi--the impersonalist or voidist who believes that the Supreme has no form.

Moksha--liberation from material existence.

Murti--a Deity of the Lord or spiritual master that is worshiped.

Narayana--the four-handed form of the Supreme Lord.

Om or *Omkara*--*pranava*, the transcendental *om mantra*, generally referring to the attributeless or impersonal aspects of the Absolute.

Paramahamsa--the highest level of self-realized devotees of the Lord.

Paramatma--the Supersoul, or localized expansion of the Lord.

Parampara--the system of disciplic succession through which transcendental knowledge descends.

Prakriti--matter in its primordial state, the material nature.

Prana--the life air or cosmic energy.

Pranayama--control of the breathing process as in astanga or raja-yoga.

Pranava--same as *omkara*.

Prasada--food or other articles that have been offered to the Deity in the temple and then distributed amongst people as the blessings or mercy of the Deity.

Prema--matured love for Krishna.

Puja--the worship offered to the Deity.

Pujari--the priest who performs worship, *puja*, to the Deity.

Purusha or *Purusham*--the supreme enjoyer.

Raja yoga--the eightfold yoga system.

Ramachandra--an incarnation of Krishna as He appeared as the greatest of kings.

Ramayana--the great epic of the incarnation of Lord Ramachandra.

Rasa--an enjoyable taste or feeling, a relationship with God.
Shabda-brahma--the original spiritual vibration or energy of which the *Vedas* are composed.
Sac-cid-ananda-vigraha--the transcendental form of the Lord or of the living entity which is eternal, full of knowledge and bliss.
Sadhana--a specific practice or discipline for attaining God realization.
Sadhu--Indian holy man or devotee.
Samadhi--trance, the perfection of being absorbed in the Absolute.
Samsara--rounds of life; cycles of birth and death; reincarnation.
Sanatana-dharma--the eternal nature of the living being, to love and render service to the supreme lovable object, the Lord.
Sankirtana-yajna--the prescribed sacrifice for this age: congregational chanting of the holy names of God.
Sannyasa--the renounced order of life, the highest of the four *ashramas* on the spiritual path.
Satya-yuga--the first of the four ages which lasts 1,728,000 years.
Shaivites--worshipers of Lord Shiva.
Shakti--energy, potency or power, the active principle in creation. Also the active power or wife of a deity, such as Shiva/Shakti.
Shastra--the authentic revealed scripture.
Shiva--the benevolent one, the demigod who is in charge of the material mode of ignorance and the destruction of the universe. Part of the triad of Brahma, Vishnu, and Shiva who continually create, maintain, and destroy the universe. He is known as Rudra when displaying his destructive aspect.
Smriti--the traditional Vedic knowledge "that is remembered" from what was directly heard by or revealed to the *rishis*.
Sravanam--hearing about the Lord.
Srimad-Bhagavatam--the most ripened fruit of the tree of Vedic knowledge compiled by Vyasadeva.
Sruti--scriptures that were received directly from God and

Glossary

transmitted orally by brahmanas or *rishis* down through succeeding generations. Traditionally, it is considered the four primary *Vedas*.

Svami--one who can control his mind and senses.

Tapasya--voluntary austerity for spiritual advancement.

Tirtha--a holy place of pilgrimage.

Upanishads--the portions of the *Vedas* which primarily explain philosophically the Absolute Truth. It is knowledge of Brahman which releases one from the world and allows one to attain self-realization when received from a qualified teacher. Except for the *Isa Upanishad*, which is the 40th chapter of the *Vajasaneyi Samhita* of the *Sukla* (*White*) *Yajur-veda*, the *Upanishads* are connected to the four primary *Vedas*, generally found in the *Brahmanas*.

Vaikunthas--the planets located in the spiritual sky.

Vaishnava--a worshiper of the Supreme Lord Vishnu or Krishna and His expansions or incarnations.

Vedanta-sutras--the philosophical conclusion of the four *Vedas*.

Vedas--generally means the four primary *samhitas;* the *Rig, Yajur, Sama,* and *Atharva*.

Vishnu--the expansion of Lord Krishna who enters into the material energy to create and maintain the cosmic world.

Vrindavana--the place where Lord Krishna displayed His village pastimes 5,000 years ago, and is considered to be part of the spiritual abode.

Vyasadeva--the incarnation of God who appeared as the greatest philosopher who compiled all the *Vedas* into written form.

Yajna--a ritual or austerity that is done as a sacrifice for spiritual merit, or ritual worship of a demigod for good *karmic* reactions.

Yantra--a machine, instrument, or mystical diagram used in ritual worship.

Yuga-avataras--the incarnations of God who appear in each of the four *yugas* to explain the authorized system of self-realization in that age.

REFERENCES

The following is a list of all the authentic Vedic and religious texts that were used, researched, referred to or directly quoted to explain or verify all the knowledge and information presented in this book.

Agni Purana, translated by N. Gangadharan, Motilal Banarsidass, Delhi, 1984
Atharva-veda, translated by Devi Chand, Munshiram Manoharlal, Delhi, 1980
Bhagavad-gita As It Is, translated by A. C. Bhaktivedanta Swami, Bhaktivedanta Book Trust, New York/Los Angeles, 1972
Bhagavad-gita, translated by Swami Chidbhavananda, Sri Ramakrishna Tapovanam, Tiruchirappalli, India, 1991
The Song of God, Bhagavad-gita, translated by Swami Prabhavananda and Christopher Isherwood, New America Library, New York, 1972
Bhakti-sandarbha sankhya
Brahma Purana, edited by J.L.Shastri, Motilal Banarsidass, Delhi 1985
Brahmanda Purana, edited by J.L.Shastri, Motilal Banarsidass, 1983
Brahma-samhita, translated by Bhaktisiddhanta Sarasvati Gosvami Thakur, Bhaktivedanta Book Trust, New York/Los Angeles,
Brahma-Sutras, translated by Swami Vireswarananda and Adidevananda, Advaita Ashram, Calcutta, 1978
Brihad-vishnu Purana
Brihan-naradiya Purana
Brihadaranyaka Upanishad
Caitanya-caritamrita, translated by A. C. Bhaktivedanta Swami, Bhaktivedanta Book Trust, Los Angeles, 1974
Caitanya Upanisad, translated by Kusakratha dasa, Bala Books, New York, 1970
Chandogya Upanishad

References

Garbha Upanishad
Garuda Purana, edited by J. L. Shastri, Motilal Barnasidass, Delhi, 1985
Hari-bhakti-vilasa
Jiva Gosvami's Tattvasandarbha, Stuart Mark Elkman, Motilal Banarsidass, Delhi, 1986
Kali-santarana Upanishad
Katha Upanishad
Kaushitaki Upanishad
Kurma Purana, edited by J. L. Shastri, Motilal Banarsidass, Delhi, 1981
Linga Purana, edited by J. L. Shastri, Motilal Banarsidass, Delhi, 1973
Mahabharata, translated by C. Rajagopalachari, Bharatiya Vidya Bhavan, New Delhi, 1972
Mahabharata, Kamala Subramaniam, Bharatiya Vidya Bhavan, Bombay, 1982
Matsya Purana
The Law of Manu, [*Manu-samhita*], translated by Georg Buhlerg, Motilal Banarsidass, Delhi, 1970
Minor Upanishads, translated by Swami Madhavananda, Advaita Ashram, Calcutta, 1980; contains Paramahamsopanishad, Atmopanishad, Amritabindupanishad, Tejabindupanishad, Sarvopanishad, Brahmopanisad, Aruneyi Upanishad, Kaivalyopanishad.
Narada-pancaratra
Narada Purana, tr. by Ganesh Vasudeo Tagare, Banarsidass, Delhi, 1980
Narada Sutras, translated by Hari Prasad Shastri, Shanti Sadan, London, 1963
Narada-Bhakti-Sutra, A. C. Bhaktivedanta Swami, Bhaktivedanta Book Trust, Los Angeles, 1991
Padma Purana, tr. by S. Venkitasubramonia Iyer, Banarsidass, Delhi, 1988
Hymns of the Rig-veda, tr. by Griffith, Motilal Banarsidass, Delhi, 1973
Samnyasa Upanisads, translated by Prof. A. A. Ramanathan, Adyar Library, Madras, India, 1978; contains Avadhutopanisad, Arunyupanisad, Katharudropanisad,

> Kundikopanisad, Jabalopanisad, Turiyatitopanisad, Narada-parivrajakopanisad, Nirvanopanisad, Parabrahmopanisad, Paramahamsa-parivrajakopanisad, Paramahamsopanisad, Brahmopanisad, Bhiksukopanisad, Maitreyopanisad, Yajnavalkyopanisad, Satyayaniyopanisad, and Samnyasopanisad.

Sixty Upanisads of the Vedas, by Paul Deussen, translated from German by V. M. Bedekar and G. B. Palsule, Motilal Banarsidass, Delhi, 1980; contains Upanishads of the Rigveda: Aitareya and Kausitaki. Upanisads of the Samaveda: Chandogya and Kena. Upanisads of the Black Yajurveda: Taittiriya, Mahanarayan, Kathaka, Svetasvatara, and Maitrayana. Upanisads of the White Yajurveda: Brihadaranyaka and Isa. Upanisads of the Atharvaveda: Mundaka, Prasna, Mandukya, Garbha, Pranagnihotra, Pinda, Atma, Sarva, Garuda; (Yoga Upanisads): Brahmavidya, Ksurika, Culik, Nadabindu, Brahma-bindu, Amrtabindu, Dhyanabindu, Tejobindu, Yoga-sikha, Yogatattva, Hamsa; (Samnyasa Upanisads): Brahma, Samnyasa, Aruneya, Kantha-sruti, Paramahamsa, Jabala, Asrama; (Shiva Upanisads): Atharvasira, Atharva-sikha, Nilarudra, Kalagnirudra, Kaivalya; (Vishnu Upanisads): Maha, Narayana, Atmabodha, Nrisimhapurvatapaniya, Nrisimhottara-tapaniya, Ramapurvatapaniya, Ramottaratapaniya. (Supplemental Upanisads): Purusasuktam, Tadeva, Shiva-samkalpa, Baskala, Chagaleya, Paingala, Mrtyu-langala, Arseya, Pranava, and Saunaka Upanisad.

Sri Isopanisad, translated by A. C. Bhaktivedanta Swami, Bhaktivedanta Book Trust, New York/Los Angeles, 1969

Srimad-Bhagavatam, translated by A. C. Bhaktivedanta Swami, Bhaktivedanta Book trust, New York/Los Angeles, 1972

Srimad-Bhagavatam MahaPurana, translated by C. L. Goswami, M. A., Sastri, Motilal Jalan at Gita Press, Gorkhapur, India, 1982

Twelve Essential Upanishads, Tridandi Sri Bhakti Prajnan Yati, Sree Gaudiya Math, Madras, 1982. Includes the *Isha,*

References

Kena, Katha, Prashna, Mundaka, Mandukya, Taittiriya, Aitareya, Chandogya, Brihadaranyaka, Svetasvatara, and *Gopalatapani Upanishad* of the Pippalada section of the *Atharva-veda.*

Upadesamrta (Nectar of Instruction), translated by A. C. Bhaktivedanta Swami, Bhaktivedanta Book Trust, New York/Los Angeles, 1975

The Upanishads, translated by Swami Prabhavananda and Frederick Manchester, New American Library, New York, 1957; contains Katha, Isha, Kena, Prasna, Mundaka, Mandukya, Taittiriya, Aitareya, Chandogya, Brihadaranyaka, Kaivalya, and Svetasvatara Upanishads.

The Upanisads, translated by F. Max Muller, Dover Publications; contains Chandogya, Kena, Aitareya, Kausitaki, Vajasaneyi (Isa), Katha, Mundaka, Taittiriya, Brihadaranyaka, Svetasvatara, Prasna, and Maitrayani Upanisads.

Varaha Purana, tr. by S.Venkitasubramonia Iyer, Banarsidass, Delhi, 1985

Vayu Purana, translated by G. V. Tagare, Banarsidass, Delhi, India, 1987

Vishnu Purana, translated by H. H. Wilson, Nag Publishers, Delhi

Vedanta-Sutras of Badarayana with Commentary of Baladeva Vidyabhusana, translated by Rai Bahadur Srisa Chandra Vasu, Munshiram Manoharlal, New Delhi, 1979

White Yajurveda, translated by Griffith, The Chowkhamba Sanskrit Series Office, Varanasi, 1976

Yajurveda, translated by Devi Chand, Munshiram Manoharlal, Delhi, 1980

ABBREVIATIONS

Bhagavad-gita is abbreviated in this book as *Bg.*
Srimad-Bhagavatam or *Bhagavat Purana* is *Bhag.*

INDEX

Aim of life
    when misguided.... 21
Asanas
    promotes better health
    122
Atheists
    say no cause to creation
    31
Being spiritual 122
Bhakti yoga 49
Bible
    describes little about
        God. 4
    describes little of God. 4
Body
    like a chariot. 32
Body is important 2
Brahma
    approached by Indra
        andVirochana. 37
Buddhist
    scriptures mention
        rebirth. 6
Cabala
    mentions past and
        future lives.... 6
Confusioin. 77
Consciousness
    is the evidence of the
        soul.. 63
Consciousness
    determines next life. 84
Death
    is an illusion. 57
    the final test....... 83

Education
    in today's world..... 8
Enlightenment
    the stage of........ 78
False ego
    causes attachment to the
        body........ 42
Fear of death. 30
Freedom
    wherever you go. .. 66
Freedom from the illusion1.2
Happiness
    from the senses. ... 27
Human body
    its true purpose. ... 35
Illusion
    materialistic
        consciousness. 11
Indra
    approaches Brahma. 37
Jesus
    not able to teach all he
        had. 3
    said there would be
        more knowledge
        to receive..... 4
Karma
    helps create future lives
    86
Koran. 5
    turn to God.. 5
Liberation
    from material existence
    81
Living entities

Index

how they get what they deserve...... 71
Material body
   a temporary vehicle. 56
Material world
   a perverted reflection. 32
Mind
   causes happiness & distress...... 42
Mundane logic
   can be a subtle trap. 56
Nature................ 80
Problems of material life .13
Purpose
   of religion........ 41
Purpose of life......... 29
   the ultimate........ 33
Real truth............ 28
Realizations
   different levels of. . 40
Reincarnation.......... 5
   found all over the world 6
Religions
   different in three ways. 6
Seeing the soul........ 75
Self
   free from sin....... 37
Self-realization........ 78
Sikhism
   one should serve the Supreme Soul.. 5
Simple living and high thinking..... 12
Soul
   beyond material happiness & distress...... 42
   death is an illusion.. 57

is eternal......... 52
its disposition to love.45
its spiritual needs... 21
natural ecstasy..... 34
resides in the heart.. 61
the location....... 62
the size........... 61
Soul is permanent....... 3
Spiritual bliss.......... 35
Spiritual identity
   more than your body. 2
Spiritual knowledge
   difficult to attain.... 40
Spiritual master
   should be approached 35
Spiritual perception.... 75
Spiritual practice
   must be steady..... 44
Spiritual realization
   in full............ 50
Suffering
   exists only in the illusion...... 23
   is superficial...... 24
   prime reason is ignorance.... 13
Superconsciousness
   integrating factor... 70
Supersoul............ 70
   Lord in the heart. .. 67
Supreme goal......... 65
Supreme Truth
   beyond capacity of the mind........ 44
Taoist
   texts mention rebirth. 6
Two birds
   sitting in the tree of the body........ 73

Ultimate truth
    realizations. 50
Universe
    always changing. . . 21
Wrong attachments. . . . 18
Yoga
    benefits. 122
Zohar
    mentions reincarnation 5
Zoroastrianism. 5
    worship God. 5

ABOUT THE AUTHOR

Stephen Knapp grew up in a Christian family, during which time he seriously studied the Bible to understand its teachings. In his late teenage years, however, he sought answers to questions not easily explained in Christian theology. So he began to search through other religions and philosophies from around the world and started to find the answers for which he was looking. He also studied a variety of occult sciences, ancient mythology, mysticism, yoga, and the spiritual teachings of the East. After his first reading of the *Bhagavad-gita*, he felt he had found the last piece of the puzzle he had been putting together through all of his research. Therefore, he continued to study all of the major Vedic texts of India to gain a better understanding of the Vedic science.

It is known amongst all Eastern mystics that anyone, regardless of qualifications, academic or otherwise, who does not engage in the spiritual practices described in the Vedic texts cannot actually enter into understanding the depths of the Vedic spiritual science, nor acquire the realizations that should accompany it. So, rather than pursuing his research in an academic atmosphere at a university, Stephen directly engaged in the spiritual disciplines that have been recommended for hundreds of years. He continued his study of Vedic knowledge and spiritual practice under the guidance of a spiritual master. Through this process, and with the sanction of His Divine Grace A. C. Bhaktivedanta Swami Prabhupada, he became initiated into the genuine and authorized spiritual line of the Brahma-Madhava-Gaudiya *sampradaya*, which is a disciplic succession that descends back through Sri Caitanya Mahaprabhu and Sri Vyasadeva, the compiler of Vedic literature, and further back to Sri Krishna. Through this initiation he has taken the spiritual name of Sri Nandanandana dasa. Besides being *brahminically* initiated, Stephen has also been to India numerous times and traveled extensively throughout the country, visiting all but three small states, and most of the major holy places, thus gaining a wide variety of spiritual experiences that only such places can give. He has also taken over 15,000 photos of the numerous holy places he has visited in India.

Stephen has written numerous articles, as well as books such as *The Eastern Answers to the Mysteries of Life* series, which includes:
The Secret Teachings of the Vedas,
The Universal Path to Enlightenment,
The Vedic Prophecies, and
How the Universe was Created and Our Purpose In It.

He has also written:
Toward World Peace: Seeing the Unity Between Us All,
Facing Death: Welcoming the Afterlife,
The Key to Real Happiness,
Proof of Vedic Culture's Global Existence,
Reincarnation and Karma: How They Really Affect Us,
The Heart of Hinduism, Vedic Culture: The Difference it can Make in Your Life,
The Power of the Dharma: A Short Introduction to Hinduism and Vedic Culture,
Seeing Spiritual India: A Guidebook to Temple, Holy sites, Festivals and Traditions, as well as
Crimes Against India: 1000 Years of Attacks Against Hinduism and What to do About It,
Yoga and Meditation: Their Real Purpose and How to Get Started,
Avatars, Gods and Goddesses of Vedic Culture: The Characteristics, Positions and Powers of the Hindu Divinities.

Furthermore, he has authored a novel, *Destined for Infinity*, for those who prefer lighter reading, or learning spiritual knowledge in the context of an exciting, spiritual adventure. Stephen has put the culmination of over forty years of continuous research and travel experience into his books in an effort to share it with those who are also looking for spiritual understanding.

Stephen now works full time to help preserve, protect and promote a genuine understanding of Vedic culture and Sanatana-dharma. To find out more about Stephen's books, articles, and projects, along with numerous resources, you can see his website at: http://www.stephen-knapp.com, or his blog at: http://stephenknapp.wordpress.com.

If you have enjoyed this book, or if you are serious about finding higher levels of real spiritual Truth, and learning more about the mysteries of India's Vedic culture, then you will also want to get other books written by Stephen Knapp, which include:

The Secret Teachings of the Vedas

This book presents the essence of the ancient Eastern philosophy and summarizes some of the most elevated and important of all spiritual knowledge. This enlightening information is explained in a clear and concise way and is essential for all who want to increase their spiritual understanding, regardless of what their religious background may be. If you are looking for a book to give you an in-depth introduction to the Vedic spiritual knowledge, and to get you started in real spiritual understanding, this is the book!

The topics include: What is your real spiritual identity; the Vedic explanation of the soul; scientific evidence that consciousness is separate from but interacts with the body; the real unity between us all; how to attain the highest happiness and freedom from the cause of suffering; the law of karma and reincarnation; the karma of a nation; where you are really going in life; the real process of progressive evolution; life after death—heaven, hell, or beyond; a description of the spiritual realm; the nature of the Absolute Truth—personal God or impersonal force; recognizing the existence of the Supreme; the reason why we exist at all; and much more. This book provides the answers to questions not found in other religions or philosophies, and condenses information from a wide variety of sources that would take a person years to assemble. It also contains many quotations from the Vedic texts to let the texts speak for themselves, and to show the knowledge the Vedas have held for thousands of years. It also explains the history and origins of the Vedic literature. This book has been called one of the best reviews of Eastern philosophy available.

The Universal Path to Enlightenment

This book brings together the easy and joyful principles and practices that are common to all of the major religions of the world. These are what can be used by all people from any culture or tradition for the highest spiritual progress, and to bring about a united, one world religion in a happy process of spiritual success for everyone. This is much easier to recognize than most people think, and is a way to bring down the differences, barriers and separations that seem to exist between religions.

This also presents:

- a most interesting and revealing survey of the major spiritual paths of the world, describing their histories, goals, and how they developed, which is not always what we would expect.
- the philosophical basis of Christianity, Judaism, Islam, Hinduism, Buddhism, Zoroastrianism, Jainism, Sikhism, etc., and the types of spiritual knowledge they contain.
- how Christianity and Judaism were greatly influenced by the early pre-Christian or "pagan" religions and adopted many of their legends, holidays, and rituals that are still accepted and practiced today.
- the essential teachings of Jesus.
- benefits of spiritual advancement that affect all aspects of a person's life, and the world in which we live.
- how spiritual enlightenment is the real cure for social ills.
- and, most importantly, how to attain the real purpose of a spiritual process to be truly successful, and how to practice the path that is especially recommended as the easiest and most effective for people of this age.

$19.95, 340 pages, ISBN: 1453644660.

The Vedic Prophecies:
A New Look into the Future

The Vedic prophecies take you to the end of time! This is the first book ever to present the unique predictions found in the ancient Vedic texts of India. These prophecies are like no others and will provide you with a very different view of the future and how things fit together in the plan for the universe.

Now you can discover the amazing secrets that are hidden in the oldest spiritual writings on the planet. Find out what they say about the distant future, and what the seers of long ago saw in their visions of the destiny of the world.

This book will reveal predictions of deteriorating social changes and how to avoid them; future droughts and famines; low-class rulers and evil governments; whether there will be another appearance (second coming) of God; and predictions of a new spiritual awareness and how it will spread around the world. You will also learn the answers to such questions as:

- Does the future get worse or better?
- Will there be future world wars or global disasters?
- What lies beyond the predictions of Nostradamus, the Mayan prophecies, or the Biblical apocalypse?
- Are we in the end times? How to recognize them if we are.
- Does the world come to an end? If so, when and how?

Now you can find out what the future holds. The Vedic Prophecies carry an important message and warning for all humanity, which needs to be understood now!

Proof of Vedic Culture's Global Existence

This book provides evidence which makes it clear that the ancient Vedic culture was once a global society. Even today we can see its influence in any part of the world. Thus, it becomes obvious that before the world became full of distinct and separate cultures, religions and countries, it was once united in a common brotherhood of Vedic culture, with common standards, principles, and representations of God.

No matter what we may consider our present religion, society or country, we are all descendants of this ancient global civilization. Thus, the Vedic culture is the parent of all humanity and the original ancestor of all religions. In this way, we all share a common heritage.

This book is an attempt to allow humanity to see more clearly its universal roots. This book provides a look into:

- How Vedic knowledge was given to humanity by the Supreme.
- The history and traditional source of the Vedas and Vedic Aryan society.
- Who were the original Vedic Aryans. How Vedic society was a global influence and what shattered this world-wide society. How Sanskrit faded from being a global language.
- Many scientific discoveries over the past several centuries are only rediscoveries of what the Vedic literature already knew.
- How the origins of world literature are found in India and Sanskrit.
- The links between the Vedic and other ancient cultures, such as the Sumerians, Persians, Egyptians, Romans, Greeks, and others.
- Links between the Vedic tradition and Judaism, Christianity, Islam, and Buddhism.
- How many of the western holy sites, churches, and mosques were once the sites of Vedic holy places and sacred shrines.
- The Vedic influence presently found in such countries as Britain, France, Russia, Greece, Israel, Arabia, China, Japan, and in areas of Scandinavia, the Middle East, Africa, the South Pacific, and the Americas.
- Uncovering the truth of India's history.
- How there is presently a need to plan for the survival of Vedic culture.

This book is sure to provide some amazing facts and evidence about the truth of world history and the ancient, global Vedic Culture. This book has enough startling information and historical evidence to cause a major shift in the way we view religious history and the basis of world traditions.

$20.99, 431 pages, ISBN: 978-1-4392-4648-1.

Toward World Peace: Seeing the Unity Between Us All

This book points out the essential reasons why peace in the world and cooperation amongst people, communities, and nations have been so difficult to establish. It also advises the only way real peace and harmony amongst humanity can be achieved.

In order for peace and unity to exist we must first realize what barriers and divisions keep us apart. Only then can we break through those barriers to see the unity that naturally exists between us all. Then, rather than focus on our differences, it is easier to recognize our similarities and common goals. With a common goal established, all of humanity can work together to help each other reach that destiny.

This book is short and to the point. It is a thought provoking book and will provide inspiration for anyone. It is especially useful for those working in politics, religion, interfaith, race relations, the media, the United Nations, teaching, or who have a position of leadership in any capacity. It is also for those of us who simply want to spread the insights needed for bringing greater levels of peace, acceptance, unity, and equality between friends, neighbours, and communities. Such insights include:

- The factors that keep us apart.
- Breaking down cultural distinctions.
- Breaking down the religious differences.
- Seeing through bodily distinctions.
- We are all working to attain the same things.
- Our real identity: The basis for common ground.
- Seeing the Divinity within each of us.
- What we can do to bring unity between everyone we meet.

This book carries an important message and plan of action that we must incorporate into our lives and plans for the future if we intend to ever bring peace and unity between us.

$6.95, 84 pages, ISBN: 1452813744

Facing Death
Welcoming the Afterlife

Many people are afraid of death, or do not know how to prepare for it nor what to expect. So this book is provided to relieve anyone of the fear that often accompanies the thought of death, and to supply a means to more clearly understand the purpose of it and how we can use it to our advantage. It will also help the survivors of the departed souls to better understand what has happened and how to cope with it. Furthermore, it shows that death is not a tragedy, but a natural course of events meant to help us reach our destiny.

This book is easy to read, with soothing and comforting wisdom, along with stories of people who have been with departing souls and what they have experienced. It is written especially for those who have given death little thought beforehand, but now would like to have some preparedness for what may need to be done regarding the many levels of the experience and what might take place during this transition.

To assist you in preparing for your own death, or that of a loved one, you will find guidelines for making one's final days as peaceful and as smooth as possible, both physically and spiritually. Preparing for deathcan transform your whole outlook in a positive way, if understood properly. Some of the topics in the book include:

- The fear of death and learning to let go.
- The opportunity of death: The portal into the next life.
- This earth and this body are no one's real home, so death is natural.
- Being practical and dealing with the final responsibilities.
- Forgiving yourself and others before you go.
- Being the assistant of one leaving this life.
- Connecting with the person inside the disease.
- Surviving the death of a loved one.
- Stories of being with dying, and an amazing near-death-experience.
- Connecting to the spiritual side of death.
- What happens while leaving the body.
- What difference the consciousness makes during death, and how to attain the best level of awareness to carry you through it.

Published by iUniverse.com, $13.95, 135 pages, ISBN: 978-1-4401-1344-4

Destined for Infinity

Deep within the mystical and spiritual practices of India are doors that lead to various levels of both higher and lower planes of existence. Few people from the outside are ever able to enter into the depths of these practices to experience such levels of reality.

This is the story of the mystical adventure of a man, Roman West, who entered deep into the secrets of India where few other Westerners have been able to penetrate. While living with a master in the Himalayan foothills and traveling the mystical path that leads to the Infinite, he witnesses the amazing powers the mystics can achieve and undergoes some of the most unusual experiences of his life. Under the guidance of a master that he meets in the mountains, he gradually develops mystic abilities of his own and attains the sacred vision of the enlightened sages and enters the unfathomable realm of Infinity. However, his peaceful life in the hills comes to an abrupt end when he is unexpectedly forced to confront the powerful forces of darkness that have been unleashed by an evil Tantric priest to kill both Roman and his master. His only chance to defeat the intense forces of darkness depends on whatever spiritual strength he has been able to develop.

This story includes traditions and legends that have existed for hundreds and thousands of years. All of the philosophy, rituals, mystic powers, forms of meditation, and descriptions of the Absolute are authentic and taken from narrations found in many of the sacred books of the East, or gathered by the author from his own experiences in India and information from various sages themselves.

This book will prepare you to perceive the multi-dimensional realities that exist all around us, outside our sense perception. This is a book that will give you many insights into the broad possibilities of our life and purpose in this world.

Published by iUniverse.com, 255 pages, $16.95, ISBN: 0-595-33959-X.

Reincarnation and Karma: How They Really Affect Us

Everyone may know a little about reincarnation, but few understand the complexities and how it actually works. Now you can find out how reincarnation and karma really affect us. Herein all of the details are provided on how a person is implicated for better or worse by their own actions. You will understand why particular situations in life happen, and how to make improvements for one's future. You will see why it appears that bad things happen to good people, or even why good things happen to bad people, and what can be done about it.

Other topics include:
- Reincarnation recognized throughout the world
- The most ancient teachings on reincarnation
- Reincarnation in Christianity
- How we transmigrate from one body to another
- Life between lives
- Going to heaven or hell
- The reason for reincarnation
- Free will and choice
- Karma of the nation
- How we determine our own destiny
- What our next life may be like
- Becoming free from all karma and how to prepare to make our next life the best possible.

Combine this with modern research into past life memories and experiences and you will have a complete view of how reincarnation and karma really operate.

Published by iUniverse.com, 135 pages, $13.95, ISBN: 0-595-34199-3.

Vedic Culture
The Difference It Can Make In Your Life

The Vedic culture of India is rooted in Sanatana-dharma, the eternal and universal truths that are beneficial to everyone. It includes many avenues of self-development that an increasing number of people from the West are starting to investigate and use, including:

- Yoga
- Meditation and spiritual practice
- Vedic astrology
- Ayurveda
- Vedic gemology
- Vastu or home arrangement
- Environmental awareness
- Vegetarianism
- Social cooperation and arrangement
- The means for global peace
- And much more

Vedic Culture: The Difference It Can Make In Your Life shows the advantages of the Vedic paths of improvement and self-discovery that you can use in your life to attain higher personal awareness, happiness, and fulfillment. It also provides a new view of what these avenues have to offer from some of the most prominent writers on Vedic culture in the West, who discovered how it has affected and benefited their own lives. They write about what it has done for them and then explain how their particular area of interest can assist others. The noted authors include, David Frawley, Subhash Kak, Chakrapani Ullal, Michael Cremo, Jeffrey Armstrong, Robert Talyor, Howard Beckman, Andy Fraenkel, George Vutetakis, Pratichi Mathur, Dhan Rousse, Arun Naik, Parama Karuna Devi, and Stephen Knapp, all of whom have numerous authored books or articles of their own.

For the benefit of individuals and social progress, the Vedic system is as relevant today as it was in ancient times. Discover why there is a growing renaissance in what the Vedic tradition has to offer in *Vedic Culture*.

Published by iUniverse.com, 300 pages, $22.95, ISBN: 0-595-37120-5.

The Heart of Hinduism:
The Eastern Path to Freedom, Empowerment and Illumination

This is a definitive and easy to understand guide to the essential as well as devotional heart of the Vedic/Hindu philosophy. You will see the depths of wisdom and insights that are contained within this profound spiritual knowledge. It is especially good for anyone who lacks the time to research the many topics that are contained within the numerous Vedic manuscripts and to see the advantages of knowing them. This also provides you with a complete process for progressing on the spiritual path, making way for individual empowerment, freedom, and spiritual illumination. All the information is now at your fingertips. Topics:

- A complete review of all the Vedic texts and the wide range of topics they contain. This also presents the traditional origins of the Vedic philosophy and how it was developed, and their philosophical conclusion.
- The uniqueness and freedom of the Vedic system.
- A description of the main yoga processes and their effectiveness.
- A review of the Vedic Gods, such as Krishna, Shiva, Durga, Ganesh, and others. You will learn the identity and purpose of each.
- You will have the essential teachings of Lord Krishna who has given some of the most direct and insightful of all spiritual messages known to humanity, and the key to direct spiritual perception.
- The real purpose of yoga and the religious systems.
- What is the most effective spiritual path for this modern age and what it can do for you, with practical instructions for deep realizations.
- The universal path of devotion, the one world religion.
- How Vedic culture is the last bastion of deep spiritual truth.
- Plus many more topics and information for your enlightenment.

So to dive deep into what is Hinduism and the Vedic path to freedom and spiritual perception, this book will give you a jump start. Knowledge is the process of personal empowerment, and no knowledge will give you more power than deep spiritual understanding. And those realizations described in the Vedic culture are the oldest and some of the most profound that humanity has ever known.

Published by iUniverse.com, 650 pages, $35.95, ISBN: 0-595-35075-5.

The Power of the Dharma
An Introduction to Hinduism and Vedic Culture

The Power of the Dharma offers you a concise and easy-to-understand overview of the essential principles and customs of Hinduism and the reasons for them. It provides many insights into the depth and value of the timeless wisdom of Vedic spirituality and why the Dharmic path has survived for so many hundreds of years. It reveals why the Dharma is presently enjoying a renaissance of an increasing number of interested people who are exploring its teachings and seeing what its many techniques of Self-discovery have to offer.

Herein you will find:
- Quotes by noteworthy people on the unique qualities of Hinduism
- Essential principles of the Vedic spiritual path
- Particular traits and customs of Hindu worship and explanations of them
- Descriptions of the main Yoga systems
- The significance and legends of the colorful Hindu festivals
- Benefits of Ayurveda, Vastu, Vedic astrology and gemology,
- Important insights of Dharmic life and how to begin.

The Dharmic path can provide you the means for attaining your own spiritual realizations and experiences. In this way it is as relevant today as it was thousands of years ago. This is the power of the Dharma since its universal teachings have something to offer anyone.

Published by iUniverse.com, 170 pages, $16.95, ISBN: 0-595-39352-7.

Seeing Spiritual India
A Guide to Temples, Holy Sites, Festivals and Traditions

This book is for anyone who wants to know of the many holy sites that you can visit while traveling within India, how to reach them, and what is the history and significance of these most spiritual of sacred sites, temples, and festivals. It also provides a deeper understanding of the mysteries and spiritual traditions of India.

This book includes:
- Descriptions of the temples and their architecture, and what you will see at each place.
- Explanations of holy places of Hindus, Buddhists, Sikhs, Jains, Parsis, and Muslims.
- The spiritual benefits a person acquires by visiting them.
- Convenient itineraries to take to see the most of each area of India, which is divided into East, Central, South, North, West, the Far Northeast, and Nepal.
- Packing list suggestions and how to prepare for your trip, and problems to avoid.
- How to get the best experience you can from your visit to India.
- How the spiritual side of India can positively change you forever.

This book goes beyond the usual descriptions of the typical tourist attractions and opens up the spiritual venue waiting to be revealed for a far deeper experience on every level.

Published by iUniverse.com, 592 pages, $33.95, ISBN: 978-0-595-50291-2.

Crimes Against India:
And the Need to Protect its Ancient Vedic Traditions

1000 Years of Attacks Against Hinduism and What to Do about It

India has one of the oldest and most dynamic cultures of the world. Yet, many people do not know of the many attacks, wars, atrocities and sacrifices that Indian people have had to undergo to protect and preserve their country and spiritual tradition over the centuries. Many people also do not know of the many ways in which this profound heritage is being attacked and threatened today, and what we can do about it. Therefore, some of the topics included are:

- How there is a war against Hinduism and its yoga culture.
- The weaknesses of India that allowed invaders to conquer her.
- Lessons from India's real history that should not be forgotten.
- The atrocities committed by the Muslim invaders, and how they tried to destroy Vedic culture and its many temples, and slaughtered thousands of Indian Hindus.
- How the British viciously exploited India and its people for its resources.
- How the cruelest of all Christian Inquisitions in Goa tortured and killed thousands of Hindus.
- Action plans for preserving and strengthening Vedic India.
- How all Hindus must stand up and be strong for Sanatana-dharma, and promote the cooperation and unity for a Global Vedic Community.

Few people seem to understand the many trials and difficulties that India has faced, or the present problems India is still forced to deal with in preserving the culture of the majority Hindus who live in the country. This is described in the real history of the country, which a decreasing number of people seem to recall.

Therefore, this book is to honor the efforts that have been shown by those in the past who fought and worked to protect India and its culture, and to help preserve India as the homeland of a living and dynamic Vedic tradition of Sanatana-dharma (the eternal path of duty and wisdom).

Available from iUniverse.com. 370 pages, $24.95, ISBN: 978-1-4401-1158-7.

Yoga and Meditation Their Real Purpose and How to Get Started

Yoga is a nonsectarian spiritual science that has been practiced and developed over thousands of years. The benefits of yoga are numerous. On the mental level it strengthens concentration, determination, and builds a stronger character that can more easily sustain various tensions in our lives for peace of mind. The assortment of *asanas* or postures also provide stronger health and keeps various diseases in check. They improve physical strength, endurance and flexibility. These are some of the goals of yoga.

Its ultimate purpose is to raise our consciousness to directly perceive the spiritual dimension. Then we can have our own spiritual experiences. The point is that the more spiritual we become, the more we can perceive that which is spiritual. As we develop and grow in this way through yoga, the questions about spiritual life are no longer a mystery to solve, but become a reality to experience. It becomes a practical part of our lives. This book will show you how to do that. Some of the topics include:

- Benefits of yoga
- The real purpose of yoga
- The types of yoga, such as Hatha yoga, Karma yoga, Raja and Astanga yogas, Kundalini yoga, Bhakti yoga, Mudra yoga, Mantra yoga, and others.
- The Chakras and Koshas
- Asanas and postures, and the Surya Namaskar
- Pranayama and breathing techniques for inner changes
- Deep meditation and how to proceed
- The methods for using mantras
- Attaining spiritual enlightenment, and much more

$17.95, 240 pages, 32 illustration, ISBN: 1451553269

Avatars, Gods and Goddesses of Vedic Culture

The Characteristics, Powers and Positions of the Hindu Divinities

Understanding the assorted Divinities or gods and goddesses of the Vedic or Hindu pantheon is not so difficult as some people may think when it is presented simply and effectively. And that is what you will find in this book. This will open you to many of the possibilities and potentials of the Vedic tradition, and show how it has been able to cater to and fulfill the spiritual needs and development of so many people since time immemorial. Here you will find there is something for everyone.

This takes you into the heart of the deep, Vedic spiritual knowledge of how to perceive the Absolute Truth, the Supreme and the various powers and agents of the universal creation. This explains the characteristics and nature of the Vedic Divinities and their purposes, powers, and the ways they influence and affect the natural energies of the universe. It also shows how they can assist us and that blessings from them can help our own spiritual and material development and potentialities, depending on what we need.

Some of the Vedic Divinities that will be explained include Lord Krishna, Vishnu, Their main avatars and expansions, along with Brahma, Shiva, Ganesh, Murugan, Surya, Hanuman, as well as the goddesses of Sri Radha, Durga, Sarasvati, Lakshmi, and others. This also presents explanations of their names, attributes, dress, weapons, instruments, the meaning of the Shiva lingam, and some of the legends and stories that are connected with them. This will certainly give you a new insight into the expansive nature of the Vedic tradition.

$17.95 retail, 230 pages, 11 black & white photos, ISBN: 1453613765, EAN: 9781453613764.

www.Stephen-Knapp.com

Be sure to visit Stephen's web site. It provides lots of information on many spiritual aspects of Vedic and spiritual philosophy, and Indian culture for both beginners and the scholarly. You will find:

- All the descriptions and contents of Stephen's books, how to order them, and keep up with any new books or articles that he has written.
- Reviews and unsolicited letters from readers who have expressed their appreciation for his books, as well as his website.
- Free online booklets are also available for your use or distribution on meditation, why be a Hindu, how to start yoga, meditation, etc.
- Helpful prayers, mantras, gayatris, and devotional songs.
- Over a hundred enlightening articles that can help answer many questions about life, the process of spiritual development, the basics of the Vedic path, or how to broaden our spiritual awareness. Many of these are emailed among friends or posted on other web sites.
- Over 150 color photos taken by Stephen during his travels through India. There are also descriptions and 40 photos of the huge and amazing Kumbha Mela festival.
- Directories of many Krishna and Hindu temples around the world to help you locate one near you, where you can continue your experience along the Eastern path.
- Postings of the recent archeological discoveries that confirm the Vedic version of history.
- Photographic exhibit of the Vedic influence in the Taj Mahal, questioning whether it was built by Shah Jahan or a pre-existing Vedic building.
- A large list of links to additional websites to help you continue your exploration of Eastern philosophy and Vedic culture.
- A large resource for vegetarian recipes, information on its benefits, how to get started, ethnic stores, or non-meat ingredients and supplies.
- A large "Krishna Darshan Art Gallery" of photos and prints of Krishna and Vedic divinities. You can also find a large collection of previously unpublished photos of His Divine Grace A. C. Bhaktivedanta Swami.

This site is made as a practical resource for your use and is continually being updated and expanded with more articles, resources, and information. Be sure to check it out.

Made in the USA
San Bernardino, CA
14 May 2014